STORIES FROM MY OCCUPATIONAL THERAPY CAREER

MARGRET KINGREY

STORIES FROM MY OCCUPATIONAL THERAPY CAREER

MARGRET KINGREY

Kravitz and Sons LLC
204 E Arlington Blvd. Suite B
Greenville, NC 27858

Published by Kravitz and Sons LLC.

ISBN: 979-8-89639-633-8 (sc)
ISBN: 979-8-89639-632-1 (e)

Library of Congress Control Number: 2026905400

Table of Contents

Stories from my Occupational Therapy Career ©

By

Margret Kingrey

Special Note to Readers

Occupational therapy (OT) can turn lives around. Thousands of people are helped every day by an OT's careful testing, observations, recommendations, and practical guidance. Yet OT is still a somewhat hidden medical profession. I would like to explain who we are and what we do.

I spent nearly forty years as an occupational therapist and was fortunate to complete training just before the big OT boom. In the following pages, I will explain that boom, discuss the need for OT, and review some of the patients I helped. Let me begin with my personal background.

I learned about occupational therapy from an older cousin's husband when I was only nine years old. Laurel Nelson was a World War II veteran and one of the first graduates at the University of Puget Sound in Tacoma, Washington. He described work that was intriguing and stayed with me. For years I thought about Laurel and how he helped his patients. The results he described were so magical that I wanted to do the same things.

My personal life interrupted a straightforward plan. Yet I remained determined. Eventually, I realized my dream. I became an occupational therapist at the age of thirty-seven. From there I worked in faraway places and with people who enriched my life in so many ways.

I was delighted to help patients through occupational therapy and found the work both rewarding and inspiring. Seeking adventure, I moved from Washington to Alaska in 1986. My occupational therapy continued there, and to my surprise, I got married again in 1989. My husband, Everett, was transferred to Alamogordo, New Mexico, by the U.S. Air Force. When he left the service and began finishing his electrical engineering degree, we moved to Las Cruces, New Mexico. We lived there until he graduated. I also attended New Mexico State University and received a master's degree in Early Childhood Special Education. This degree qualified me to teach in an occupational therapy program at the University of Texas in El Paso. When Everett graduated, we moved to Bolton, Massachusetts, in 1997 and then to Upper Marlboro, Maryland, in 2000. Five years later we moved to Carver, Massachusetts, just west of Plymouth. In 2008 we moved to Ellettsville, Indiana. Then in 2016, we moved to Blair, Nebraska. Each relocation was related to my husband's job.

Because we moved frequently, I changed jobs often. As you read this book, you'll see that my work experience involved patients of many ages and diagnoses. I treated patients with many diagnoses. I worked with disabled children in outpatient clinics and school districts. I helped older patients in nursing homes, outpatient facilities, and in home health. I also collaborated with clients from a variety of cultures and even worked with those who did not speak English.

Most of the time I was a hands-on staff therapist. However, after earning the Master of Arts in Early Childhood Special Education at New Mexico State University in 1996, I joined the faculty at the University of Texas in El Paso, Texas, to teach in their new occupational therapy department. I taught in two other OT programs, one in Massachusetts and one in Maryland. Although I began a doctorate in occupational science at Towson University, I did not finish that degree. But each experience enriched me and the patients I helped. I spent nearly forty years as an occupational therapist and proudly cited some of my experiences in this book.

For privacy reasons, client names were changed, except for one. (I will review why later.) Client locations remain true and took me from the Arctic Circle to far south and then to the east coast and Midwest.

Two of my stories are published elsewhere; however, the copyrights belong to me. One story is included in an out-of-print book.

I hope that readers will gain an appreciation of the breadth and scope of Occupational Therapy. We work to help clients return to work but also to actively improve everything that a person does from the time they get up in the morning until they go to bed at night. We evaluate complex physical and mental capacities. Each activity we direct helps our patients live full, independent, happy, and productive lives. Our work changes patients' lives and enhances interaction with family, friends, and community.

INTRODUCTION

The first time I ever heard about Occupational Therapy was in 1950 when my much older cousin, Lucille, and her husband, Laurel Nelson, came to spend a few days with us at Thanksgiving. Laurel was a veteran who had returned from the Pacific theater after WWII and studied Occupational Therapy at the University of Puget Sound in Tacoma, Washington. He and one other man were the only men in the newly started OT program at the University of Puget Sound.

When Laurel watched me working on a copper tooling project, he said I would make a good OT. I was only nine years old. I asked him what an Occupational Therapist did, and he explained that OTs helped people do all kinds of things. "Think about everything you do during the day from the time you get up until you go to bed," he said. "Occupational therapists help their clients do everything they need to do during the day, from getting dressed, taking a shower, working, cooking meals, and playing games. They work with people who have physical and mental health problems and children who have cerebral palsy and other disabilities, too." Laurel knew I liked a lot of different things. I also like helping people. I began talking about Occupational Therapy with anyone who would listen and always explained that my cousin's husband was an Occupational Therapist.

On May 10, 1971, Washington State passed House Bill 90, which mandated that all "handicapped children…be insured an appropriate educational opportunity…" This legislation was an amendment to previous legislation passed in 1969 that included education for children with handicapping conditions but did not specify how those services would be implemented. House Bill 90 detailed how the mandate for education would be provided to those children, the opportunities parents or legal guardians would have to advocate for their children should their child be denied services, and how school districts could acquire services for children either through hiring their own therapists or contracting with clinics. Children in the county court system would not be removed from the court system to attend local schools without the permission of the court, however.

This legislation sets up requirements for all school districts within the state of Washington. Services are now available in speech-language therapy, occupational therapy, and physical therapy for identified students. Treatment must be based on professional evaluations and recommendations. Those services would either be provided by the school districts directly or through contracts with appropriate agencies. Services could be provided within the school, or a student could be transported at school expense to an appropriate clinic. The law was to be implemented by July 1, 1973. This legislation placed high demand for physical, occupational, and speech therapists within the state.

In the fall of 1973, I was admitted to the University of Puget Sound on probation, as my grades from Grays Harbor Community College in 1960 were not the best. I was one of four "non-traditional" students accepted into the School of Occupational Therapy. "Non-traditional" meant that I was not a recent high school graduate. I already had an Associate of Arts degree. I was in my early thirties, divorced with a six-year-old son. The other "non-traditional" students were also older women who were married, and two of them had children. There were several men in our class who were veterans from the Vietnam War.

During my education, I went through some tough times. The first was that my son started the first grade and was not doing well. He did not like the school, nor his teacher, and he had difficulty reading. He also had problems with fine motor skills, probably brought on by the spinal meningitis he suffered when he was four years old. Meningitis had lingering effects. It would take some trials and time before I found a better setup for my treasured Fritz.

And there were other challenges during my studies. After my first semester, I took a class on Aging and the Aged during the winter term. Simultaneously, my mother had a stroke and was hospitalized for several days, then was transported from Aberdeen, Washington, near my parents' home in Hoquiam, Washington, to Tacoma General Hospital. There, she was treated by doctors in the neurology department. She died on Sunday evening at Tacoma General. We were heartbroken. My father called to ask me to arrange for an Episcopal priest we knew in Tacoma to prepare the funeral in Shelton, Washington, where most of our family lived. Both my parents were born and raised in Shelton. I was grateful that the faculty and the friends I made at the University of Puget Sound and in our neighborhood were very supportive during that time. My friends at Trinity Episcopal Church were also kind and understanding.

At the end of my son's second-grade year, the Tacoma Public Schools opened the district so that children could attend different schools outside their neighborhoods. I found a school downtown that seemed like a good fit for him. Fritz and I went to a meeting and decided to enroll him in McKinley Grade School. Eight-year-old Fritz would have to ride the public bus that stopped just a block from our apartment. This was a big, grown-up responsibility for him. Transportation to and from school was free. He enjoyed that school, and the teachers accommodated his difficulties. Fritz had spinal meningitis when he was four, and when I was studying neurology later,

I realized his illness had created some difficulties in his brain function for fine motor coordination. This created problems with handwriting. Fortunately, Fritz did quite well in the new school and made several lifelong friends there.

My challenges continued in the classroom. During my education at the University of Puget Sound, there were some changes in the curriculum, and I was in a couple of classes that I had no background for. Those were classes in crafts and woodshops. It was not the crafts or woodworking that was the problem, but the application to different disabilities, which I had not yet studied. I asked questions when I did not know about a specific disability. My eagerness to understand irritated some of the students who already had taken classes in those areas. I knew my questions bothered some of the younger students. They sighed and rolled their eyes. But I did not care and asked questions anyway. I also became aware that my main interest was to work with children. And later I learned that age and life experiences were beneficial. My insistence on appreciating the relationship of tasks to disabilities really helped my future patients.

My father had not been feeling well in June of 1974, and when I talked with him one day, I told him he should visit the doctor and find out what was wrong. Shortly after that chat, he took my advice. After his appointment, he called to say he was diagnosed with colon cancer. In November 1974, he underwent surgery to remove his colon and part of his liver and pancreas. The surgeon was upset that there was so much cancer in Dad's internal organs. The surgeon yelled at me because he was so upset with what he found. Dad had chemotherapy and was in the hospital for nearly three months. He never did quit work, as he had so much vacation time built up. He said he would not retire.

In early 1975, Dad went to stay with his brother in Shelton. His brother's wife was a former nurse who could take care of him. When Dad got stronger, he moved into the cabin he built at Arcadia Point, just outside of Shelton. Our cousin, Lucille, Laurel's wife, lived up the road, and she often drove him for radiation treatment in Olympia. She cooked meals for him at the cabin or at her house and brought them to the cabin.

I made trips to Shelton from Tacoma as often as I could, but with school and my son's activities, it wasn't more than once a month. Again, the faculty and my friends were very supportive. I tried hard not to talk about my father's illness too often and focused on getting through the assignments at school. Suddenly, Dad was in the clinic at Shelton for a week, and then he died in November 1975. He was 64 and had never officially quit working.

On November 29, 1975, President Gerald Ford signed into law Public Law 94-142, which was called the "Individuals with Disabilities Education Act,' often referred to as IDEA." This legislation was closely aligned with the law already on the books in Washington State and increased the demand for occupational therapists across the country.

Just a month after President Ford's new law, I graduated. At my graduation in December 1975, my sisters and one of my maternal aunts attended the ceremony. A former boyfriend who lived in California also came to the graduation. I was delighted to see them all. I held onto my new diploma and met most of them at my apartment to celebrate and have something to eat. Later, Fritz and I planned an additional celebration at a new pizza place called "Pizza and Pipes," not far from our apartment. It was just the two of us. We wanted to celebrate together after the three years of struggles we had been through. But we weren't finished yet. Struggles continued.

I still had two clinical affiliations of three months each to do. I also had to take and pass the national certification examination for occupational therapy before I could work as an occupational therapist. The required clinical affiliations included one in mental health and one in physical rehabilitation. Fritz had to finish grade school and move on to junior high. Both of my affiliations were close to Tacoma so that we did not have to move. I did not want Fritz to have to change schools.

Sandi, my older sister, was the executor of Dad's estate, and she got busy with all the paperwork. After several months, the estate was settled, and I had enough money to pay off my student loans, buy a better car, and start looking for a house in Tacoma. The apartment we lived in was sold, and we needed to move. My inheritance allowed me to do an optional affiliation for three months in pediatrics. That was the area I wanted to work in. In April 1976, I took the National Occupational Therapy Certification Examination. I passed, but just barely. I was also nearly finished with my mandatory affiliations. I was ready to take some time off before starting my pediatric affiliation in the fall of 1976.

That summer, Fritz and I took a trip to Disneyland and then up to San Francisco. We visited Alcatraz, rode a streetcar, and enjoyed some fun time together.

Surprisingly, after my pediatric clinical at the Children's Therapy Unit in Puyallup in the fall of 1976, I could not find a job. I applied for jobs in several school districts around Tacoma. I applied at both Tacoma General Hospital and Mary Bridge Children's Hospital. No jobs were open. I did not want to move Fritz out of the Tacoma Public Schools or away from his good friends. I was getting desperate.

Fortunately, we stayed in the apartment until I completed the pediatric affiliation at Good Samaritan Hospital in the Children's Therapy Unit. Just after I finished that affiliation, the real estate agent with whom I had been looking at houses came to the apartment and said, "I found you a house!" It was the week before Christmas. We drove to the house on Washington Street, one block from the University of Puget Sound campus, off Union Avenue. It was a perfect location. I still had enough money to put a down payment on the house, and within a week the deal was signed. In January, Fritz and I moved in. I still did not have a job! My faith that we would stay in Tacoma was confirmed. I was determined. I would get a job somewhere.

Chapter 1

I knew Liz from my days at Grays Harbor Community College. She called me one evening shortly after Fritz and I moved into our new house. Liz was twenty years older than me, but somehow, we had a lot in common. We both liked to write and studied literature together. We ate lunch together most days at college years ago.

"How would you like to come work as my assistant in the Weyerhaeuser advertising department?" she asked. "I know you were always interested in writing and acting, but I hear you have a degree in occupational therapy. Sally told me you couldn't find a job." Liz looked out for me. She knew that both of my parents had died during my days at the University of Puget Sound. Her husband worked for Weyerhaeuser doing property tax work. He and my father worked together to get timber tax laws in Washington changed for the benefit of timber companies.

"Oh, gosh. I need a job. If I come to work at Weyerhaeuser, I will still be looking for work in occupational therapy. If that won't be a problem, I can start right away."

"Great! You can start Monday. Be here at 8 a.m. sharp. We work from 8 until 4:30 with half an hour for lunch. I'm in an office in the building on the left of the main headquarters. You can park in the parking lot in front of our building. See you then."

The following Monday I arrived before eight. The janitor let me in. Liz came into the office right at eight. "I will show you around and introduce you to a few people. Here's your desk. I have some things for you to go through laid out on it already, and I'll show you what I need you to do."

My desk was in a hallway not far from Liz's office door. I could look out at the front door and see who was coming and going from the building. Across the hall from my desk was an open area where several of the people from the accounting department worked.

The first few months went well. Liz and I enjoyed working together. She was very supportive. Then one day in June, a friend of mine asked me if I would babysit his dog while he went home to Hawaii. I said I would be happy to do that. He dropped Ace off at my house on Saturday before he left for the airport. Ace got along well with Fritz and me. We had known Brian and Ace since my days at the University of Puget Sound.

Then one morning, I was getting ready for work, and I let Ace outside do his thing. We did not have a fenced yard. When I went to get Ace back into the house, he was nowhere to be found. I called and called for him. Finally, I jumped into the car and drove over to Brian's house just a few blocks away. There was Ace resting on the front porch. I put him into the car and realized I could not get him back to my house and be at work when I was supposed to be. I headed to the office.

It was going to be a warm day in early June. I could not let Ace stay in the car, so I brought him into the building. We walked past a man in the accounting department. "What are you doing bringing that dog into the office?" he demanded. I explained the situation and told him I could not leave Ace in the car as it would be too hot. I told Ace to stay under my desk and went to find a bowl for some water, which I put near the wall beside my desk.

I got ready for a presentation. People gathered, and the conference room was full. The slogan Liz and I decided upon had the word “mobile” in it. However, when the slide appeared on the screen, the word was spelled “mobil”. Right away, our guests spotted the misspelling. I was called to task. I apologized and said I would take care of that misspelling within the week. (This was in the days of slower technology.) That timeframe was unacceptable to them. Liz also apologized and said she would take care of it herself, and she would handle their advertising from then on and take me off the job.

As soon as the meeting was over, I returned to my desk. I was very upset with that error. Then my phone rang. “I want to see you in my office immediately,” the head of the advertising department told me. His office was in the main building on the Weyerhaeuser campus. I walked over to his office and knocked on his door.

“Come in,” he said. He was obviously upset. “How could you show a presentation with an error in it?” he demanded.

“I’m sorry,” I said. “I just missed seeing it, and Liz was too busy to check my work before the presentation. She said she trusted me.”

“Well, not only did you disgrace our advertising department, but bringing that dog to work and into the office was also against everything we stand for. We are not your home. I want you to pack up your personal belongings and leave. Don’t ever come back either. You’re fired.”

I was near tears. Leaving his office to walk back to get my things and get Ace into the car took all my strength. I told Liz what happened. “I know. The director called me to let me know he fired you. I’m sorry. Nothing I could say would change his mind.” She helped me carry some of my stuff to the car. As I got Ace into the back seat, Liz and I hugged each other. “I’ll see you sometime,” she said. “I hope you can find an OT job.”

I left Weyerhaeuser and drove home dabbing my eyes and blowing my nose. I did not know what I would do next. I prayed that somehow another job would come my way. At least I still had money in my savings account, and being so close to the university, maybe I could rent a room to a college student.

I rearranged my life. Fritz and I spent another summer together. I planted a vegetable garden in the backyard. Brian returned from Hawaii and picked up Ace. "I have some teenagers I'm training. How about letting them paint the outside of your house? You buy the paint, and we'll do the work at no charge." I agreed.

"Brian, there's a tree in the front yard that needs to be cut down. I noticed that it is rotting in spots, and I'm afraid that in a winter storm it could fall and ruin my neighbor's fence, and maybe his porch, depending on how it falls. Do you know anyone who might be able to cut it down and use the wood for firewood?"

"Yes, I know just the person. Beth's husband can do that. He used to work as a lumberjack, so I know he's aware of how to do that kind of thing safely. He can also split the wood with you so you will get some firewood for your fireplace, too."

I kept applying for OT positions in the Tacoma area. I even applied for a job in the Bremerton school district which was not that far across the Narrows Bridge from Tacoma. I also applied for work in the Mason County School District. I thought if worse came to worse, we could live at the cabin on Puget Sound just outside Shelton, and I could sell the house in Tacoma. Fritz would just have to make the adjustment. I prayed that we would not need to move.

Chapter 2

Beginning My OT Career

In August 1977, I got a call from Linda, the director of the Children's Therapy Unit in Puyallup, asking me if I would be interested in a job there. I would begin the last week of August, just before the school year started. The job would focus on occupational therapy evaluations and therapy for children in five local school districts four days a week. I would be at the clinic one day a week to attend staff meetings and provide therapy for several children there. I did not mind having to bounce around from school to school. I knew the territory because I worked at some of those schools while on my affiliation. Linda knew that I wanted to expand my knowledge in the area of learning disabilities and autism and to become certified in administering the Southern California Sensory Integration Test (SCSIT). That was a special test developed by A. Jean Ayres, Ph.D., OTR in California. SCSIT tested children in areas of balance, touch, vision, memory, and infant reflexes that may still affect functioning in movement.

Just before I graduated in December 1975, Public Law 94-142, the Education for All Handicapped Children Act, passed in the U. S. Congress. President Gerald Ford signed the legislation into law. There was very little difference between the law Washington State already had on the books and had been implementing since 1973. But now, between the Washington State law and the new federal legislation, the demand for therapists in the schools soared. The timing was perfect for me to find my preferred practice area.

The job at the Children's Therapy Unit was a perfect fit. I already knew the therapists who worked there. I knew the plans Linda developed for expanding therapy services within the clinic itself. She and the director of the hospital were already making plans to renovate and add space to the unit. As their caseload grew, she needed some therapists to work more hours in the clinic itself, rather than in the school districts. That was how she came to think of me and offer me the job, which I grabbed immediately. My OT career was finally underway!

Chapter 3

Sammy

Learning to advocate for clients or students was not an easy experience. I never took lessons in how to make an effective argument. I was never a member of a debate team. Although I often tried to make a point with classmates, I was more likely to work hard to understand their point of view rather than fight for my own. One afternoon at a school district we served, the Director of Special Education asked about a youngster I evaluated and recommended for therapy.

Sammy was a seven-year-old who had difficulty with fine motor coordination. He had retained infantile reflexes that should have been integrated during his infancy. Let me explain. When babies are about four months old, they begin to extend their arm on the face side when they turn their head. This action helps to develop eye-hand coordination. The arm stretches out so that the infant can see their hand. When they wiggle their fingers, they make the connection in their brains that the wiggling thing belongs to them, and they learn to control the fingers to grasp objects. As this reflex, called the "asymmetrical tonic neck reflex" (ATNR), becomes integrated into the body/brain system,the baby can bring the hand toward the face without automatically turning the face away. If this reflex is not well-integrated into the nervous system, the child can become stressed when keeping the head still as the hand comes to the center of the body. This stress causes tension and fatigue when doing tasks at midline, or tabletop activities, which require eye-hand coordination.

Sammy was disruptive in the classroom because he had difficulty sitting still to do tabletop activities. He was likely to be held back a grade because he was not keeping up in reading or writing. His arithmetic papers were never finished either.

My argument with the Director of Special Education was that with just six to nine months of occupational therapy to get his ATNR integrated and fine motor skills developed, Sammy would be well on his way to doing very well in school. He was smart enough, according to the school psychologist. I was sure Sammy also needed a chair where he could put his feet flat on the floor or some footstool, so his feet did not dangle from the chair. His seating was inadequate to give him a sense of stability when he worked at his desk.

"I could probably have that child functioning within normal limits in six months," I bragged. "Then he would be doing OK in the classroom and no longer need any services. He wouldn't be disruptive to other students, either." I realized I was practically shouting at the Director of Special Education because I was so distraught that he would not let me put Sammy on my schedule.

"The law is written the way it is, and we need to comply with the law," was his response. "It is not written for those with minimal problems but for those with the most difficulties. Furthermore, if you mention to the parents at the parent conference what you have just told me, the school district may have to pay for outpatient services. So, don't mention it. I agree with you; the legislation could have been written better by Congress and the state legislature, but it was not, so we just need to do what the law says."

"Well, whoever wrote that wasn't thinking straight! They obviously didn't know they could save kids a lot of distress by getting them help," I retorted. I apologized for raising my voice while making my point. He laughed. "That's OK. I love a good argument. And I often don't get many, especially from staff."

We shook hands, and I went on to see a child who was severely mentally retarded.

How Sammy's parents learned about what I had said about their son needing some OT, I will never know. However, it was shortly after my outburst with the Director of Special Education that Sammy turned up at the outpatient clinic. I did another evaluation and got a prescription from his doctor to treat him. It was good that the parents were attentive and caring and had medical insurance that would help pay for therapy.

Some of the activities we did in therapy included wheelbarrow walking, riding the scooter board down a ramp to hit a target, drawing on the blackboard, and working with playdough. I cooked homemade playdough for my clients in those days. They usually took some home so they could continue working with it whenever they wanted. We also began sessions with Sammy lying prone in a suspended swing, either throwing beanbags at a target or spinning around and stopping on a word I had written on pieces of paper placed on the floor. The activities varied and were usually fun at each session.

(Wheelbarrow walking is an activity where the child gets down on the floor on their hands and knees. Another person, usually a parent or older sibling, holds the child's ankles and lifts their legs off the floor. Then the child uses his hands and arms to move forward. The pressure on the arms and shoulders helps integrate an infantile reflex that may not have been well integrated when the child was an infant. Once the reflex becomes more integrated, the child experiences less stress when doing activities that require their hands to work at the middle of their body.)

Therapy work is not always smooth. Within three months, Sammy seemed to be doing worse in behavioral control. I knew this was not unusual, as the brain was trying to make new pathways and was accommodating a different organization of connections. We needed to keep the therapy going to make those new connections permanent. After another month of therapy, Sammy made another adjustment. He became a compliant, cheerful youngster who was doing much better in school. He could sit still at his desk to work on tabletop activities. His reading improved because he could hold a book at midline without feeling stressed. By now the ATNR was fully integrated, and his printing had improved.

After six months of therapy, Sammy was doing very well in school and getting along better with his siblings at home, and his mother commented that he even ate without spilling food on the floor. I had not known that he did that before we began therapy because she had never mentioned it. His parents and teachers were relieved that he was doing so well. The school provided Sammy with a stool for his feet to help him feel more stable while doing tabletop activities. I felt gratified that my predictions to the Director of Special Education had indeed turned out to be true. I was able to discharge Sammy at the end of just over six months of therapy.

Chapter 4

More Learning

When I began my clinical affiliation in pediatrics, I learned how to administer several formal tests. These included the Peabody Developmental Motor Scales, the Purdue Peg Board Test, the Bruininks-Oseretsky Test of Motor Proficiency, and the Bayley Scales of Infant Development. For these evaluations, I read the manual, gave the test several times under the observation of my supervisor, and did the scoring, which she then reviewed. The other evaluation techniques I learned were to closely observe patients while they did specific tasks. I also used my intuition. Although most occupational therapists are cautioned not to use their intuition, and mine was sometimes wrong, I felt my sensitivity to others was invaluable in developing a well-rounded picture of the whole person. I was older than the other therapists at the clinic and also a parent. Those experiences made me feel my intuition and observational skills might be a bit more relevant to some of the clients we served. The one evaluation I wanted to learn to help my patients was the Southern California Sensory Integration Tests (SCSIT). None of the occupational therapists at the clinic were trained in that evaluation.

I needed special training for the Southern California Sensory Integration Tests (SCSIT). The training consisted of two full days, one day of lectures and one day of test administration techniques. Those of us in training were then instructed to administer three tests to clients from age four to eight, write up a report on each client tested, and have that report evaluated along with the test scores. The SCSIT is very rigid in the way it is administered. There was specific wording, positioning of the administrator and client, and the order in which each section of the test was given. Deviation from any of these aspects of the test would invalidate the scores.

The SCSIT tested for visual perception, eye-hand coordination, tactile perception, and vestibular system functioning. The vestibular system is a set of semicircular canals within the inner ear. Fluid in the inner ear moves against tiny hairs in the canals when the head is moved. These hairs send messages to our brains that tell us where our head is in space. That sensation coordinates with our eye gaze for the horizon (upright position) and the information from our muscles and joints (called proprioception) to keep us in an upright position for walking, etc. These three systems are needed for balance. When one system gives faulty information, or there is a lack of information from one system, our balance and orientation in space can be poor. Think of when you have an ear infection and how you sometimes feel that you are unsteady on your feet until the infection goes away, and you can understand how some people who have vestibular dysfunction feel all the time. When you are a child, you may accept your situation as "normal" and think everyone feels the same way.

When I learned that training for the SCSIT would be given at the University of Washington in Seattle, I immediately signed up for the weekend and paid the course fee. In 1978, continuing education credits were tax-deductible. After states passed laws requiring licensure for occupational therapists, a specific number of continuing education credits became necessary to maintain one's license to practice in the state.

I drove to Seattle early on a Saturday morning and listened to the college faculty deliver the lectures. The following day, we were trained in the administration of the tests, the clinical observations, and the scoring procedures. After passing that part of the training, I returned to the clinic, where I administered the test to three clients, scored the tests, and wrote a report on each. We were given three months to finish that process. The test scores and reports were sent to the Ayres Clinic in California, where they were graded.

Part of the reason I loved the SCSIT was that it was the only evaluation that OTs could use that was based on both developmental neurology and child development. Dr. Ayres, who developed the test, believed that some lack of development of what were called "lower brain areas," meaning those parts of our brain that develop more automatic functions such as the sense of balance, touch, integration of infantile reflexes, etc., was the basis for skills such as balance, eye-hand coordination, body awareness, and attention. I believed she was right, based on my experience with my son and his difficulties with fine motor coordination. I wanted to learn more to help children like Fritz.

When my grades came back from California, I saw plus scores on two of the tests and reports but flunked on one of the reports. I would not be certified to administer the SCSIT. I was devastated! I analyzed the paperwork. Where had I gone wrong? I saw it. I had stated explicitly the location in the brain where the problem was. I had crossed a medical line. That determination was not within my realm of practice. That kind of diagnosis was for a pediatric neurologist with a medical doctor's degree to make. I only had a Bachelor of Science degree, so I was overstepping my area of expertise.

The next time training in the SCSIT was held at the University of Washington, I took the course again and passed without difficulty. I was careful to write my test results within the parameters expected. Since the clinic now had an OT who was certified to administer the SCSIT, we began receiving several referrals for children needing to be tested using that specific examination. I was the only therapist in the clinic who was certified to administer the SCSIT.

I was also called upon to talk about the test to other clinicians, including physicians. I spoke about the test itself and how it applied to children with learning disabilities and those suspected of having autism. My talks were often given to pediatricians and family practice doctors as well as to the school psychologists. I even gave a lecture to lawyers and judges who worked for the Pierce County Juvenile Court system. I was able to explain how the SCSIT applied to children with sensory-motor difficulties that often led to learning disabilities and behavioral problems. I also explained how the sensory systems could be applied to therapy for those diagnosed with autism.

I usually did one or two evaluations per week using the SCSIT. The testing itself took one and a half to two hours per child. The scoring took another hour, and the report could take another one to two hours. There was always a follow-up appointment with parents to determine a treatment plan and schedule therapy. A doctor's order had to be obtained before therapy could begin unless the original order from the doctor was written to "…evaluate and treat as necessary." As pediatricians became familiar with what was involved in the testing, report, etc., they often just wrote the order to treat as necessary when ordering the evaluation.

The school districts were beginning to hire their own occupational therapists. Each school district needed less time from other therapists. Each school year, I worked more days in the clinic. As my time at the clinic increased, I evaluated more children using the SCSIT who needed treatment. I was required to travel less and less to different school districts.

My clinical clients began to include a wider range of diagnoses. I was now seeing children with learning disorders and mental retardation as well as children with cerebral palsy.

I was co-treating with both the speech therapist and physical therapists from time to time and was given the job as clinical supervisor for OT students who were doing their twelve-week clinical affiliations. I was trying to keep up with new developments by attending conferences and workshops as well.

My son, Fritz, was doing well in his new school. He was moving along every year and getting better grades. The teachers would still criticize him for his handwriting but not as much as when he was in the other grade school. He had friends in the neighborhood. He often spent weekends with friends. He rode his bike, which seemed to be his way of dealing with his feelings. We made a routine of getting pizza for dinner on Sunday evenings and then watching "60 Minutes" on TV before bed.

Fritz was growing. He soon was taller than I was. His father was over six feet tall, and I knew that Fritz would be as well. Fritz was an outgoing fellow and had numerous friends. One of them lived across the street, and they often got together in a room above our garage after school. They would play board games there and talk about their school experiences. They also loved to ride bikes together. Other neighborhood friends came to our house in the evening or on weekends to watch football games on TV. Once Fritz and a friend had me help them dress for a Halloween party. I got out a couple of sheets and made costumes so they looked like Roman royalty. Fritz said later that they were the only two Romans there, and they enjoyed being different.

Chapter 5

Betsy

Most of the children I evaluated were compliant with the testing, no matter which evaluation I used. However, some were not. Those are the children I most often remember. Soon after I was officially certified to evaluate children using the SCSIT (Southern California Sensory Integration Test). I was scheduled to evaluate Betsy, a five-year-old. Her mother, Martha, brought Betsy to the clinic.

The Children's Therapy Clinic in Puyallup had been remodeled, giving us a wonderful testing space where there were no distractions. The room was small with a one-way mirror so parents could watch from another small room. The child could not see their parents, but the parents could observe the child and me during parts of the tests.

I met Betsy and Martha in the clinic's waiting area. As I introduced myself to them, Martha shook my hand, but Betsy looked at me out of the corner of her blue eyes. Her blond curly hair was held back with pink barrettes on either side of the part. She just seemed a bit shy. Martha and I chatted for a few minutes, then we all walked down a hall to the evaluation room, where I had the test materials waiting on the table. I explained to Betsy that her mother would be sitting in the little room we walked through to get to the testing room. Betsy came with me into the testing room without making a fuss.

I often did not know why the doctor had written the prescription for the SCSIT evaluation. Most of the doctors who wrote these 'scripts' knew I preferred not to have any preconceived ideas before an evaluation. Since many of the doctors had information on what the SCSIT was evaluating from the talks I had given, they were looking for objective test results. Sometimes the physicians would ask me to call them with my initial impressions before they received the written report.

The first part of the SCSIT had two plastic blocks and a form board with a peg placed in it. The child selected which block fit into the board like a jigsaw puzzle. Several of these puzzles tested visual perception and allowed the administrator to observe the child's eye-hand coordination.

Betsy did the first three items in the block test, then she stopped. She sat and glared at me. I was at a loss as to what to do next. There was a certain script that I had to follow to administer the test correctly and get verifiable results. I decided to administer the vestibular test and go on to some clinical observations. In the test of vestibular function, the child sat on a small board that was turned several times and then stopped. The child's eye movements were timed to show how fast the child could accommodate to the spinning. The board was spun in one direction, then the other direction. Betsy participated in that test easily.

We left the small testing area to do some of the clinical observations. Martha came along with us and sat at a small table in the large treatment room. I asked Betsy to walk on a balance beam, hop on one foot, and skip. She did not know how to skip. When I asked Betsy to get onto her hands and knees to test for the ATNR, she again refused. I looked at Martha. She smiled and asked Betsy to get down on her hands and knees. Betsy did as her mother asked, but when I walked over to Betsy, she quickly stood up. Martha and I decided we would try doing the rest of the testing on another day. Betsy obviously was done doing anything I asked her to do for now, and our scheduled time was over. I had another patient waiting.

The following week, Betsy and her mother returned to the clinic. Betsy again refused to comply with the more formal testing. I directed her to do some other activities, which included riding on a scooter board down a ramp to knock over a pile of cardboard blocks, drawing on the blackboard, and playing in the ball bath. I tried again to engage her in the formal testing in the treatment room instead of the testing room, but she would not cooperate. I could not figure out how to get her to do the more formal testing. With just some of the test results, I had information about the fact that she had difficulty with balance and seemed to be hypersensitive to light touch. I felt she could benefit from therapy. However, I had no real scores, except for the test of vestibular function, which was low. I told Martha I would call the referring physician and talk with him, then get back to her. Martha apologized for Betsy's behavior and said she was concerned that she would do the same thing at school. Martha did not want Betsy to have problems when she started kindergarten in a few weeks.

I called the physician later that day. "Did you notice how much Betsy looks like Martha?" the doctor asked.

"No, not really," I replied.

"I think there's a genetic component at work here," he said. "Schedule another session with them and look closely at them. Make some comparisons, then instead of trying to test Betsy, let her play while you talk to Martha about her school experience. I'm going to write an order to treat Betsy and send it over."

I called Martha, and we scheduled another appointment. When she and Betsy entered the clinic, I immediately saw what the physician had observed. Other than hair color, Betsy looked like Martha. Betsy was blond, while Martha was brunette; their eyes were the same shape and color, slightly wide-set. Their noses were nearly alike, somewhat broad, and their mouths were also broad with thick lips. Even their hand gestures were similar. I was impressed with the physician's observational skills.

We all went back to the treatment area, where Betsy played in the ball bath, drew on the blackboard, and colored at the desk while I asked Martha about her school experience.

"Oh, I had a terrible time in school. I couldn't sit still, my handwriting was awful, and I hated arithmetic. I was not able to focus until the teacher read stories. I loved being read to, even though I didn't like reading myself. I was always watching other children and what they were doing."

"Was all your schooling like that?"

"Well, no. About the seventh grade, there were more kids, and we moved from class to class, I seemed to settle down a bit. I barely graduated high school, though, and got married right after graduation. Other kids teased me a lot, too. I just don't want Betsy to have those problems, if I can help it."

"The doctor has sent over a prescription to treat Betsy," I told her. "I believe that therapy is needed to help her with her attention span, her balance, and being less sensitive to light touch. I don't have scores on some tests to prove that; I only have observations and those of the doctor. Would you like to have Betsy treated on a trial basis? We can see her two times a week for six months to see if her behavior and sensory processing improve. I will not be the treating therapist. I have already talked with another therapist who will treat her."

"Yes, I do want to try anything, so she won't have the same problems I had. I sure hope therapy will do the trick," Martha said.

We scheduled the appointments, and Betsy began working with another OT. Within a few months, Betsy was much improved in her ability to attend to tasks, allow light touch, and walk the balance beam. She loved the ball bath activities and working on the blackboard, as well as spinning in the hammock swing. She was totally compliant with the treating therapist.

I had an opportunity to chat with Martha in the waiting area one afternoon. She told me that Betsy was doing well in kindergarten. Martha seemed very happy that Betsy was on her way to enjoying school and making friends there. "The teacher seems to understand that Betsy needs to move around sometimes. She sends Betsy to the office with notes during class time. Betsy says it makes her feel important."

"Did Betsy ever tell you why she wouldn't do the more formal testing with me?" I asked.

"No, she never did, but then I never asked her either. She loves coming here now for therapy," Martha said.

I never figured out why Betsy was noncompliant during testing, but then she was not the only child I tried to test who was like that.

Betsy taught me to quickly change my approach when testing other noncompliant children. Some of those children would return to the testing room after doing clinical observations in the large treatment area. Betsy also taught me to be a bit more observant as well.

Chapter 6

Patrick

A referral came to the Children's Therapy Unit for a six-year-old boy who had a seizure disorder and apparent behavioral problems. According to the information accompanying the referral, Patrick's seizures were well-controlled by medication. However, he was exhibiting difficulties getting dressed on time for school, eating meals with the family, and sitting still in school. Dr. Steve, the referring pediatric neurologist, wanted me to test the child using the SCSIT, since it would be the best test to demonstrate if Patrick had other neurological problems. The doctor had done brain scans, but in the early 1980's, neither the computerized tomography (CT) scans nor the magnetic resonance imaging (MRI) machines were as developed as they are currently.

When I first met Patrick, he looked like most of the children I saw, a perfectly normal-looking kid. His light brown hair was a bit long. His blue eyes were bright. He seemed interested in his surroundings as he scanned the waiting room area while he sat next to his mother. Ruth was a woman who appeared to be in her mid-thirties. She had the same color hair as Patrick, but her eyes were more green than blue. She was slight of build, about five and a half feet tall. She was dressed in a skirt and a plaid blouse. She was a teacher.

"Hi, I'm Margret," I said, extending my hand to Ruth.

"Hi, I'm Ruth, and this is Patrick," she said as she stood up and turned slightly toward Patrick. He stood up and shook my hand, too.

"What are we going to do?" he asked immediately.

"Well, first I'm going to give your mom some papers to fill out, and then we're going to go to a room where you and I will do some work," I handed Ruth a clipboard with several sheets of patient information to fill out.

"What kind of work? Do I have to take off my clothes? Are you a doctor?" Patrick was obviously not shy.

"We'll do some puzzles and stuff like that, then we'll go into a big room, and you can walk on a balance beam, draw some pictures, and things like that. No, you don't have to take your clothes off, maybe just your shoes and socks. And, no, I'm not a doctor. I'm a therapist."

"OK. Let's go," Patrick said, pulling on his mother's arm. We headed down the hall with Patrick walking beside me. Ruth held the clipboard in one hand and walked slightly behind us, holding onto Patrick's shoulder with the other hand.

"He's always up for new things," Ruth said, somewhat apologetically.

"Great! I like new things too."

We entered the room where parents could watch through the one-way window. I told Ruth that she could sit there and fill out the paperwork while Patrick and I entered the testing room. "Your mom will be right here on the other side of that mirror. She can see what we're doing, but we won't be able to see her. Isn't that cool?"

I told Patrick what we would be doing, and then we both sat down at the table with me sitting across from him. The first item of the SCSIT was already on the table. It was a block design test. Patrick went through all the visual perceptual parts of the test without any problems. Then he wanted to see if he could see his mother through the mirror/window. He got up and looked closely at the glass. "I can't see her," he said.

"I'm pretty sure she is still there," I told him.

"I'd better go look to make sure."

"OK, but come right back because we have more to do here," I said.

Patrick opened the door between the two rooms, and once he assured himself that his mother was still in the observation room, he came back to the table and sat down. I began the part of the test where the child is touched by the therapist on the finger while his hands are on the table. A manila folder is held above the child's hands so he cannot see where the therapist touched him. With the folder removed, the child points to where the therapist touched him. In another touch test the child is given a shape to feel while the therapist holds a paper with several shapes on it above the child's hands. Using the other hand the child points to the picture of what the shape feels like. The shape must be identified by touch only. This test allows the therapist to determine that the sense of touch is coordinating with the child's visual interpretation of the touch sensation. Patrick did well on all these tests.

When Patrick finished the tests at the table in the testing room, I took him and his mother to a large treatment room so I could observe Patrick hopping, skipping, and walking on the balance beam. I had him do the test of vestibular stimulation in the larger room as well. Patrick seemed to have difficulty with his balance and his coordination of larger body movements. He did not know how to skip and could not do that even after I had demonstrated how it was done. He always led with his right foot, followed by his left foot coming up behind the right foot, shifting his weight to the left foot and moving the right foot forward again. Hopping on one foot was also difficult for him on the left foot.

We moved on to the vestibular function test. Patrick sat on the low board, and I spun him around. After the third spin,

Patrick fell off the board onto the carpeted floor. We tried a second time, and the same thing happened. I asked Ruth, who had been sitting in a small chair watching us, if he had problems going up and down stairs. "Yes, sort of. I noticed that he always puts his right foot first and, like skipping, follows with the left foot. He doesn't fall, though."

"What else besides the difficulties with routine do you see?" I asked.

"Well, that's the biggest thing. He gets doing something and doesn't want to leave it. His teacher says the same thing happens at school, besides the fact that he doesn't like to sit in the chair for long. He will sit at home for a long time. He prefers to sit on the floor working on a project. He likes to work on projects: puzzles, blocks, and things like that."

"Hey, Patrick. How about drawing me a picture of yourself for me?" I asked. I put a piece of paper on a table that was in a corner of the treatment area and handed him a pencil. Patrick sat down and grabbed the pencil. I noticed that his pencil grip was not well-controlled. He placed the first three fingers on top of the pencil with the thumb and little finger opposing the fingers on top. This was common in children who had difficulty with fine motor coordination. I decided to do another test of fine motor coordination where the child turns over pegs in a pegboard. The Purdue Pegboard Test is timed and well-researched, so I could get a definitive score and not just rely on my observations of his fine motor abilities.

"OK, I think we're done for today," I said. "You did a great job, Patrick." I stood up and began to walk toward the door to the hall, expecting Patrick to follow, but he headed in the opposite direction.

"What's this for?" he asked, pointing to the scooter board ramp. He walked to the top of the ramp and turned to run down it.

"That's a scooterboard ramp. We have some games where children lay on one of these," I pointed to a scooter board near the ball bath in the far corner. "When I say 'Go,' the child pushes off from the wall and rides down the ramp to knock over some cardboard blocks, or something."

"Wow! I want to do that!"

"We'll see. I must figure out what we need to do first by scoring all the tests you did today."

"Oh, I hope I did bad so I can come back. That sounds like fun!"

His mother smiled. "We'll see." She handed me the paperwork. "Thank you. When will I hear?"

"Probably I'll have everything scored and written up by Thursday. You should hear by Friday. I'll call the doctor. If I recommend therapy, he will need to write a prescription for that."

After Patrick and his mother left, I felt sure that I would be seeing Patrick again. I finished scoring the tests and found Patrick had some difficulty with balance and fine motor coordination. Both were influenced by a poorly integrated infantile reflex, the ATNR (Asymmetrical Tonic Neck Reflex). In addition, from the picture of himself he drew, Patrick did not seem to have a good sense of the left side of his body. In the picture, that side of his body was smaller and somewhat distorted. There was a very small foot on his left leg. He had drawn a smile on his face, which was a good indication that he enjoyed what he was doing.

I was still puzzled by the fact that Patrick had difficulty getting himself ready for school. There was no indication that he shouldn't be able to put on his clothes all by himself, except for tying his shoes, which a lot of children his age can't do unless given specific instructions. In therapy, I could teach him how to do that easily enough. He seemed to be a bright youngster and definitely curious.

With the report written, his parents were called and came in for a conference. The recommendation was for me to treat Patrick twice a week for three months, then once a week for an additional three months. I had talked to the physician, who said he would be glad to write the prescription for the full six months. Patrick's parents were eager to start. Since both worked—she was a teacher, and he was a janitor at one of the schools—the therapy needed to be late in the day. His mother could bring him in at four o'clock. Patrick would be my last patient twice a week. I'd have to do a bit of shifting with another patient, but I didn't see a problem.

We also discussed giving Patrick a written schedule to follow on weekdays so he would get ready for school on time. Perhaps that would help motivate him and help his mother feel less likely to nag him every morning. Since she worked, she had plenty to do in the mornings without always trying to get Patrick and his younger sister ready, too. Dan, Patrick's father, thought a chart that Patrick could check off would be worth a try. He would get a check mark on the paper schedule on the mornings he was ready, and at the end of the week if Patrick had five check marks, he would decide what to eat for dinner as a reward. This was an easy behavior modification plan.

I preferred not giving parents home therapy programs, because I believed that parents who are both working, trying to run a household, and raising their children have enough to do. There were a couple of fun things I would encourage parents to do, however, especially for a child who had poorly integrated infantile reflexes, which Patrick had. Since his asymmetrical tonic neck reflex was still evident on testing, I assigned the activity of wheelbarrow walking every day to his parents.

Patrick could get ready for bed, then come to get either parent, who would wheelbarrow walk him back to his bedroom.

Using the hall as the space in which to do this activity worked well, especially in the early stages of therapy when a child often collapsed on one arm or the other. The confined space of a hallway limits potential dangers such as knocking over a table or a decorative item in the living room. It also kept the child focused because there were usually few distractions in the hallway. The wheelbarrow walking and the behavioral chart were the only things I suggested that Patrick's parents do at home. Patrick loved the wheelbarrow walking.

We scheduled therapy twice a week. I began seeing Patrick the following week. His mother brought him after school because Dan could not get time off. After school was his busy time as a janitor. After the first couple of weeks, I realized I needed to keep the activities varied frequently because Patrick did not like sitting long. This was a behavior that the teacher at school had complained about as well. Patrick liked the hammock swing for increased vestibular stimulation. He liked spinning around, but because of his seizure disorder, I kept that motion limited. He loved the scooter board activities. I varied those activities between sliding down the ramp and setting up obstacle courses in the hallway. He enjoyed writing on the blackboard more than sitting at a table to do fine motor activities such as drawing, writing, or coloring.

Generally, after six weeks of therapy, some observable changes occur. Often the child incorporates a better pencil grip when writing or wants to limit their spinning in the hammock swing. I observed that Patrick was more interested in the scooter board activities than in the swing after six weeks. His pencil grip was more consistent with the "normal" grip. The thumb and index finger were on opposite sides of the pencil, with the middle and other fingers stabilizing the pencil on the paper.

At home, he complied with the behavioral chart to get himself dressed before school, but that only worked for a couple of weeks before he slipped into his old habits. His mother and

I decided to change the motivator to money at the end of the third week. He would get a dollar to spend as he pleased on Friday if he got himself dressed for school on time every day. I also helped him learn to tie his shoes. That went well in the clinic but did not transfer to his home environment. He was still asking his mother to tie his shoes for him, and he often came home from school with his shoes untied.

I was beginning to sense that something else was going on with Patrick. I couldn't put my finger on just what that was. I talked to some of the other therapists during our weekly team meeting. The other therapists said they just saw Patrick as a regular kid when they observed him in the waiting room. The director of the department suggested I call the pediatric neurologist and discuss Patrick with him. After our team meeting, I put in a call to the physician. He called me back as I was getting ready to leave for the day.

"What are you having trouble with?" he asked.

"I don't know exactly. Patrick is a great kid to work with, and he seems to be responding well to treatment. His fine motor skills are demonstrating improvement, as is his balance, but he's different from other kids I've seen. He likes changes in our routine often. He is not responding well to the behavioral program to get himself dressed. He gets focused on something at home and hates to bother getting dressed, according to his mother. I would like to have him tested up at the Children's Clinic at the University of Washington by a child psychologist. We don't have a child psychologist here, and I would like to have the opinion of one. We can't do IQ testing either."

"Have you talked to his mother about that?"

"Well, no, not yet. I wanted to run it by you before I said anything to her."

"OK. I agree additional testing would be helpful. He's well-controlled on his medication as far as seizures are concerned.

I'll write a script and send it over to you. You can discuss your concerns with Ruth and give her the information. Then make the appointment up in Seattle at their convenience. Keep me posted."

On Thursday when Ruth and Patrick arrived for his appointment, I told Patrick that I needed to talk to his mother for a bit before he and I worked together. "Why do you need to talk to her? I want to play," Patrick demanded.

"Well, you go into the treatment room. I have some things set up for you already," I told him. "I have blocks ready for you to knock over, and I hid six things in the ball bath for you to find. I'll be in in just a few minutes, then you can get into the swing."

"OK. But just a few minutes. I don't want you cutting me short on my fun."

I smiled at him. He reminded me of my mother shaking her finger at me. Patrick went into the treatment room. I turned to Ruth. "Let's sit in the hall here for a few minutes," I said, gesturing to a couple of chairs. "Ruth, I don't want you to be alarmed, but I believe that there's something different going on with Patrick that I don't understand. I feel I need to know what it is. I talked to Dr. Steve, and we thought having Patrick take some tests at the Children's Clinic in Seattle would be good so we can get a more complete picture. We don't have a child psychologist here."

Ruth frowned and looked away. "What do you mean by 'complete picture'? Do you think there's more wrong with him?"

"Well, not exactly wrong. I think he's really smart, but I can't be sure unless I have information on that verified by a child psychologist. I also think that the Children's Clinic may be able to help with his problems of following a routine when it comes to dressing. There's got to be something else that I'm missing. Dr. Steve wrote a prescription for psychological testing and an IQ test. It's your decision. As far as I'm concerned, he's making nice progress with his fine motor skills and balance. It will be another couple of months at least until I retest him in other areas to get definitive results."

"Getting him to bed is easier since we started doing that wheelbarrow walking routine. He loves that and wants to go two or three times down the hall before bed. He knows we won't do that until he's in his pajamas. But when he gets to his bedroom, he still doesn't go to sleep like I think he should. He wants to read until at least ten o'clock. I have to go in and sit with him in the dark until he falls asleep." Her forehead was wrinkled. "I'll talk this over with Dan, but I think we will probably do what you want."

"Thank you."

"I'll call to let you know tomorrow. I can make the appointment," she added. I handed her the prescription that Dr. Steve sent over and the contact information for the Children's Clinic at the university.

We entered the treatment room. Patrick was immersed in the ball bath. "What took you so long? I found all that stuff and hid more stuff for myself. Bet you can't find it."

"I bet I can." I walked over to the ball bath and began trying to find hidden objects. "OK, tell me what I'm feeling around for, and how many things did you hide?"

"Oh, about a million crayons," Patrick laughed.

"Great. Now I'm going to have to miss my dinner to find them all," I retorted.

"No. You'll go home before you find them." He laughed again. "I'm bored. I'm going to get into the swing if you'll hang it up."

"Sounds good to me." I secured the hammock swing, placed pictures on the floor in a circle, and told him how many times to spin and which picture I wanted him to stop on. We finished the session ten minutes after our scheduled time, so Patrick did not miss any minutes. He would have told me he'd been cheated if he hadn't gotten in his full hour of therapy.

I drove home that evening worrying that I'd added an extra burden on the family for no reason. Ruth and Dan were really concerned and wanted to parent Patrick in a responsible, loving way. He was their first child. They had a little girl who was three, but she seemed to have no problems. They were thankful for that because Patrick was enough of a challenge.

Ruth called me the following afternoon to say they had made an appointment at the Children's Clinic in Seattle. The earliest they could be seen was two weeks away. They would have to cancel one of Patrick's therapy appointments with me. She said that Patrick would miss coming to therapy, but he seemed to understand he needed to go to Seattle. They promised he would miss therapy only once.

During the next session Patrick would not stay seated longer than ten minutes. Finally, I asked him what was bothering him. Why I hadn't asked that question before was beyond me.

"That chair is hard, and it hurts my butt! I don't like my butt hurting."

"OK." I walked over to a cabinet and pulled out a small foam cushion. Here try this." I placed the cushion on the seat of the chair.

Patrick sat down. "This is wonderful."

"So, let's play some cards. Then we'll do some playdough figures. How about that?"

"OK."

Patrick had sat for twenty minutes now that his butt had soft support. Maybe he should have the cushion to take to school with him. That might be his problem at school, too. I told Ruth she could take the cushion with her and ask the teacher to use it during class time.

> "I don't know why I never asked him about why he didn't sit long at school either," she laughed. "Sometimes it's the simplest things we just don't think about."

At our next session, which was near Halloween, Ruth told me that the cushion was working wonders with his restless sitting. I said she could keep the cushion as a loan, and she could encourage the school to get one of their own.

"Hey, Patrick, how would you like to make playdough today?" I was trying to encourage his interest in new things. I handed him the recipe to see if he could figure out what we needed. He read the recipe and measured the ingredients that I had put out on the counter, and then I cooked the playdough while he decided what color he wanted. He chose a combination of red and yellow.

"That makes orange, you know," he told me. "I want orange so we can make pumpkins."

"That sounds good, but we can't use this playdough until it cools off. We don't want to burn our hands. We'll do some scooter board things first." We ended the session, and Patrick took his play-dough pumpkin home with him.

The Tuesday after Patrick's appointment at the Children's Clinic, Ruth told me that they were not finished writing the report. She and Dan had a follow-up appointment in a week, so she had to cancel Patrick's appointment for the following Tuesday. I sensed that she was worried about the results, but I decided not to discuss it with her until after she and Dan went to their meeting. Perhaps it would have been better to talk with her about her concerns, but my focus was on Patrick. He was already riding the scooter board down the ramp and telling me to "get with it." At this point, Patrick was getting a bit pushy. Three months into our work together, I wasn't surprised, though. He knew the program very well by then and knew I was a willing participant in the fun we had.

The next week, I drove to work anxious about what I would learn from Ruth about the Children's Clinic evaluation. At nearly four, I went into the reception area to find Dan, Ruth, Patrick, and Marie, Patrick's little sister. They were all sitting except Marie, who was playing on the floor with some toys we kept in the waiting room. Dan stood up to shake my hand. "I'm glad you sent us up there. Ruth is going to tell you all about it. Marie and I will wait here until the session is over." He turned to Patrick. "OK, Bud, you go with Margret, and I'll see you after you're done."

Ruth, Patrick, and I walked down the hall to the treatment room. "Go ahead on in, Patrick; I put some things out on the table for you, and you can also draw on the blackboard while your mom and I talk. Please draw me a turkey, OK?"

Ruth and I sat on the chairs in the hall. "Here's the report." She handed me a folder, and then she started to cry. "I don't want to raise a genius!" she whimpered. Since I always had a pocket pack of tissues, I handed it to her and looked at the results of the Stanford Binet Intelligence Test. Patrick had scored 174 IQ points –the highest score possible on the test for a child of his age. I skimmed the other test scores. He did better on the gross motor tests of the Bruininks-Oseretsky Test of Motor Proficiency than I had gotten nearly three months prior but still placed below average. His fine motor scores were within normal limits at this point. Their clinical observations were a bit better than my own but indicated that he still needed therapy. I knew another three months of therapy would probably pull him into the normal range.

"Ruth, I'm sorry, but these scores are good. He's showing progress in what we're doing. Tell me what you're thinking."

"Dan is a genius. We don't tell people because the only job, he's able to hold down is janitor at the school. I don't want Patrick to follow the same path. I wanted just a normal, regular kid with a mild seizure disorder. Not some freak kid that can't even get himself dressed in the morning." She started crying harder. I put my arm around her shoulder and let her cry a bit longer, wondering what I was going to say next. All sorts of thoughts ran through my mind.

A couple of therapists came down the hall with small children who had cerebral palsy. The therapists looked at me with concern. "It's OK," I assured them. They turned the corner and disappeared into a large treatment area.

"Have you shared this information with the school yet?" I asked Ruth as she gained control of her tears.

"No. Do you think I should do that now? They will be testing him next year in third grade anyway," she said, blowing her nose.

"I think the sooner they know the better. Also, I think we are going to change the getting dressed chart. Changing the rewards every week, letting him choose what rewards he works for, might bring better results, and he won't be bored. I'm going to talk to a couple of people I know about working with children with higher IQs, but I won't use any names, so won't violate confidentiality. Has the Children's Clinic sent Dr. Steve a copy of this report?"

"They said they were going to. I don't know if he's gotten it yet, though."

"I'll call him tomorrow to see. I'm not planning to change Patrick's treatment schedule since I'm working more on lower brain functioning and the gross motor skills. This doesn't make any change in that, but it does give me an idea about how

I need to keep activities varied and more challenging for our remaining months together. I wish we had a child psychologist on staff so you could get some assistance and support from someone more knowledgeable than me. Our director has been interviewing, but I don't think she's hired anyone yet. What does Dan say about all this?"

"He's as stumped as I am. But he kind of shuts down when we talk about handling Patrick. And I don't know what the school is going to do."

"Well, we won't know that until they have this information. In the meantime, I'll give you whatever support I can. Please feel free to call me at home, too. I'll give you my number. I'm usually available until 9 p.m."

"Thank you, I sure wasn't expecting this. I think I'd rather have a retarded kid. I would know how to handle that," Ruth added. (In the late 1970s, teachers had more training with children with mental deficiencies than with children on the high end of the intelligence scale.)

The following day, I called Dr. Steve. He had gotten the report but hadn't had time to go over it. I gave him the results and assured him that from my perspective Patrick was doing well in OT, but with the IQ results, I believed that we needed to get the school involved in helping Patrick use his potential. Perhaps we could arrange a meeting with the district and get Patrick additional learning experiences of some kind. My biggest concern was that Patrick would get so bored he would not want to go to school anymore. My intuition was telling me that was what Ruth feared as well.

I talked to several of the other therapists who worked at the clinic, and I also went to our director to discuss Patrick's situation. She told me that she might have a child psychologist working with us in another week. If that person took the job, we might have her work with Patrick on some of the home behavior issues.

Over the weekend, I saw David Waller, a former English teacher of mine, and his wife, Jane. They had an art gallery, and I made some stained-glass ornaments for David to paint on. He sold the ornaments at his gallery. While I was there, I mentioned I had a patient with a genius IQ. He was doing great in school; except he was bored sometimes. And he couldn't seem to get dressed in the morning. David chuckled. "I had a cousin who had a similar problem," he said. "He would never get his dirty clothes in the hamper, so his mom put a basketball hoop on his closet door with the hamper underneath. My cousin would throw his clothes like a basketball. When he made a basket, his clothes ended up in the hamper instead of all over his room. You've got to make getting dressed a game."

I never thought about a game for getting dressed. Maybe Dan could think up a game that would help Patrick with the dressing problem – one smart guy helping another smart guy. It was worth a try.

On Tuesday, I mentioned to Ruth that perhaps Dan could make getting dressed fun for Patrick. We would forget the behavior modification chart for now and see if this new approach might work better. Ruth was accepting my suggestions. She had put another cushion on Patrick's chair at the dining table, and he was more willing to sit and eat with the family.

"I'm ready to try just about anything," Ruth admitted. "I have taken this whole problem on myself, and you're right, Dan should be more involved." She sounded certain that she would follow through with this new idea. She also informed me that the school district was looking at forming a "gifted class" because it discovered three other students, all from the third-grade testing that was recently completed, who also had IQs well above average. One of these students was a neighbor who knew Patrick. I told her that Dr. Steve and I talked briefly, and he just said to "keep him in the loop." Ruth and I were the communication links, and together we were making progress with plans for Patrick beyond the children's clinic treatment sessions.

After the beginning of the new year, I decided to retest Patrick informally. I had him draw a clock with the hands at ten minutes to two o'clock. He also drew another picture of himself. I wanted him to color the new pictures to see if he could stay within the lines on the left, which he hadn't done before. This was my informal observation of his visual field and motor development for the left side of his body in terms of body awareness. He also skipped with his left foot coming forward during this observational session. Although not a smooth skip, it was considerably improved in terms of right/left coordination compared to the initial testing session.

Ruth turned Patrick's dressing problem completely over to Dan. Dan was hiding Patrick's clothes and timing him to see how fast he could find each item and get dressed. It worked! Ruth was now free to make lunches and prepare Marie for day care. Ruth was feeling less stressed. She seemed relieved, too, that Dan was more engaged with parenting Patrick, especially in a fun way.

I sat down with the new pediatric clinical psychologist soon after she was hired to talk about Patrick. She seemed to think that I was doing fine, and that she did not need to get involved right now. If things changed, however, she was there to help.

In March, after nearly six months of treatment, Patrick was moved to an accelerated learning classroom with three other students. The transition was not going well for him, then he had a seizure that put him into the hospital. Dr. Steve wanted additional testing and to adjust his medications, if needed. The seizure had been a petit mal seizure, not a grand mal seizure, but it had lasted several minutes longer than any of his previous seizures. This was the first seizure Patrick had had since I became involved with his case. Dr. Steve called me to see if I had noticed any subtle changes in Patrick's performance.

"No. When I last did some informal observations, he was doing very well. Patrick demonstrated improvement in body image and skipping, and his pencil/paper skills were progressing nicely. He seems to have improved balance, too, and no longer spends much time in the hammock, swing or other vestibular-stimulating activities. That was to be expected at this stage of therapy. I started thinking about discharging him soon."

"Do you want to watch as we do the CT scan? It's scheduled for tomorrow morning if you have time. I'd like you to be there for parental support and to see how the equipment works, too, if you can. I know you've been interested in that test for a while."

"I think I can arrange that."

"Good. See you tomorrow upstairs at 7:30."

I rearranged my calendar by calling a couple of parents to change appointments and then drove home wondering how things would go in the morning. I appreciated the nearly forty-five-minute drive to and from my house in Tacoma to the clinic in Puyallup. It gave me time to gear up for the clients ahead, staff meetings, etc., and in the evening drive, I thought about making dinner and having the evening to read, write, knit, and spend time with my son. There were multiple chores to do as well, but the drive was always a welcome transition time.

Patrick spent the night at the hospital. He was wheeled into the area where he lay on a gurney to await his turn in the scanner. I chatted with him a bit. He was groggy but smiled nevertheless. Ruth came in shortly after Patrick was brought into the room. Dan and Marie were staying home waiting for a phone call from Ruth after the scan was done. The computerized tomography (CT) scanner was new to the hospital within the past year. We had heard about it being used, but none of the therapists except our director had seen the machine. It looked like a huge black cave.

As Patrick was moved into the machine, the noise was loud. It sounded like a low, growing thump, thump, as it rotated positions. Dr. Steve showed me areas of the brain he was concerned about on the screen mounted on a wall. He would compare the previous scan with these new images before he could make any conclusions. "This seizure could have been due to some new growth or connections that have been made. But that's just a guess now," he said. We watched for a bit longer, then Dr. Steve went to talk with Ruth. Before I left, I told Ruth I would see her on Thursday, but she could call me if she wanted to talk later in the evening.

Later that day, Dr. Steve phoned to tell me the comparison of the two scans showed that the area in the lower right temporal lobe was more developed than in the earlier scan. He wanted me to cut Patrick's therapy down to once every other week for the remainder of the school year and see what happened. "I think he's benefited well from therapy. There are some new neural connections. I think his brain just needs a rest. I'm going to increase his medication slightly, but the scan didn't show any growth of the tumor."

"Well, that's good news. Did you tell Ruth that you wanted to change the treatment schedule?"

"Yes. She's OK with that. She is ready for a rest, too, I think."

"She's really been a trooper. I'll make the changes on my end. Did you send down a new order?"

"Yes. It should be delivered tomorrow morning."

I called Ruth after I checked my schedule with the secretary to let her know I would not see Patrick on Thursday as planned, but I would see him at the end of the month. She seemed relieved to reduce such frequent trips to the clinic.

Near the end of the school year, Patrick had made the adjustment to both his new class schedule and therapy schedule. He was doing very well getting himself dressed for school and finally was tying his shoes himself! He even taught Marie how to tie her shoes. "She's getting to be a big girl now. She's four," Patrick explained to me.

Patrick was discharged from therapy at the end of May. He had been seizure-free since March. For our last therapy session Patrick's Draw-a-Person picture was well done. Both sides of the body in the picture were nearly equal in proportion. He drew a mustache on the man. "That's what I'll look like when I'm all grown up," he told me. He was doing well in school and Dan was encouraging Patrick to experiment on his computer at home. Ruth was feeling confident that Patrick would achieve a better life than she had originally thought after learning of his intellectual capabilities. Marie was Marie. I felt that we all had achieved our goals for Patrick.

Chapter 7

Bobby

In August 1979, Linda told us at a staff meeting that we would be providing services to some children from the nearby reservation. Four children would be bused to the clinic on Monday. Fran, one of the other occupational therapists, and I would evaluate them. After we determined what, if any, therapy was needed, the tribal council would decide if the children would receive treatment. The tribe would then contract with the hospital for the youngsters' therapy. Linda explained the contract process was lengthy. The hospital administration already decided that we would treat the children as needed despite no contract signatures. Since the hospital was a church-owned, not-for-profit hospital, I was not surprised that the hospital decided to provide services even with only a proposed contract.

I had some knowledge of the Native American cultures in the Northwest, having grown up near the Squaxin Indian Reservation and seeing the Indians fishing on Puget Sound numerous times. I dated a Native American for a while when I was in high school. He didn't live on a reservation, however. He didn't seem all that different from other boys I dated in high school. Sam was a good hunter, and we often found ducks or Canada geese on our doorstep that he and his friends shot before school.

Neither Fran nor I had ever treated children who lived on the reservation. We did not treat children from the reservation in any of our school districts either. The reservation educated the younger children in its own school until they were in ninth grade. Older children attended the local high school. Most of the standardized tests we used did not have Native American children in their test samples; however, we felt that gross motor and fine motor development should coincide with children of all ethnicities. Now we know that is not necessarily true.

The following week, four children got off the bus. They were accompanied by an aide from the reservation school. She carried four folders with school performance records and some health charts. I took the folders and went to our secretary, who made copies of everything for us. Fran and I had no time to read anything at the moment because our time with the children was limited to an hour. One of the boys displayed severe burns on his face and hands. He was missing his right ear, with scarring primarily on the right side of his face. He was missing most of his right hand. Only the ring and little finger remained. His left hand was also scarred, but all the fingers seemed to be intact.

"Why don't you test Bobby, and I'll take the other three for clinical observations, then we can switch," Fran said. (In the late 1970s and 1980s, many Native American families gave their babies names common to children in the U.S. They thought that this would make it easier for people of other ethnic groups to relate to their children and make it easier for their children to be accepted.)

"OK," I agreed. "Come with me, Bobby. We'll walk down the hall to the testing room. It's this way." I gestured toward the hall past the reception room. "So how old are you, Bobby?"

"I'm supposed to be ten."

"What grade are you in?" I asked.

"Third."

"We're going into this small room here." I opened the door to the parent's viewing area and then the door into the small testing room.

"It looks like a cell," Bobby said.

"Well, it isn't. It's just that we need to work in a quiet place with no distractions," I assured him.

As we sat down at the small table, I realized that Bobby was not comfortable being in the testing room or with the small table and chairs. He was larger than most of the children I tested, and his manner was different as well. He seemed withdrawn and guarded. He did not smile nor seem curious at all. "You know what? Let's go into another room where it's bigger, and you can see your friends," I said. "I can bring this stuff with us."

I gathered the testing materials I had laid out, and Bobby and I entered the larger treatment room where Fran was working with the other children. She gave me a quizzical look, but I just smiled and said, "We decided to work in here instead."

She continued giving instructions to the other children.

I proceeded to test Bobby with the Peabody Developmental Motor Scales. He seemed more comfortable when he was with the other children and not alone with me. His hand function was limited because of the scar tissue and missing fingers on his right hand. His dexterity on the left was below normal due to the scarring on those fingers. He had some difficulty performing on some of the gross motor tests, also. "So how much scarring do you have on your legs?" I asked.

"Oh, the right one is pretty bad, but the left one is mostly burned on the hip part. Didn't they tell you I killed my parents and little sister?" he said.

"No. They didn't tell me anything about what you did, nor how you got burned. I didn't know you had burns at all."

"Yeah. I did all that when I was five—playing with matches while my mom and dad were drunk. Isn't that what you expect me to say?"

"Bobby, I don't expect you to say anything. I just expect you to do the things I ask you to do the best way you can. OK?"

"Oh, OK."

I was glad Fran was in the room so she could overhear the conversation. We would need to discuss our experience with these youngsters when we finish our evaluations. She seemed to be having no problem with the other three children. I probably would be giving at least one of them more formal testing on their next visit, and Fran could do clinical observations with Bobby.

I decided to have Bobby get into the hammock swing and try to toss some beanbags into the ball bath across the room. Once he was settled, lying on his stomach in the swing, I handed him the first beanbag. He tried to throw it overhand. It didn't go far. I handed him another beanbag. This time he threw it underhanded with his left and hit the target. Then he began spinning fast. I let him spin for just a minute and then told him to stop. When he didn't, I said again, "STOP!" in a loud, commanding voice. He put his left hand and foot on the floor to stop the swing.

"Now everybody wants a chance to swing and spin," Fran said. "I guess we got all we can get today. It's almost time for you guys to leave." All the other children had a turn on the popular swing. I let Bobby use the scooter board to go down the ramp several times while Fran and I helped the other children. I kept my eye on what Bobby was doing and had some additional thoughts about what he and I might do in therapy. The aide came into the room and said the bus was waiting. "OK, guys," Fran said. "Everybody put your shoes on, and we'll walk to the bus."

I watched Bobby put on his tennis shoes, but he didn't even try to tie them. I wondered how well he was able to button his shirt or jacket when he needed to. I also wanted to know how well he handled cutting his food or opening a can of soda. There wasn't time for that on the first visit, so I filed those concerns for next week when they would return for the last evaluation session.

At the end of the day, Fran and I talked about what we discovered during our first time with these children. "I think the boys I saw have some sensory processing problems, but I'll know better after I do the formal testing," Fran said. "I also think they work better together."

"Well, I agree that Bobby seemed to do better when he was with the other kids. He was definitely more relaxed. But he's got some anger and control issues, too, I think. Maybe Trish, our child psychologist, can sort those things out if the tribal council will go along with a psychology evaluation. I think we should talk that over with Linda." It was getting late, and I needed to get home to fix dinner for Fritz and me.

Over the next three sessions, Bobby became my patient. Fran worked with one of the other children who we determined had a learning disability. The other two children seemed to be functioning within the average range despite the fact that they had facial characteristics that later were identified with Fetal Alcohol Syndrome by researchers at the University of Washington.

Bobby and I worked on some of his activities of daily living, such as one-handed shoe tying. I ordered a button hook so he could button his shirt by himself. We tried a rocker knife for him to use to cut meat or other food for himself, but his foster parents would not let him keep the knife. There was some concern that he might use it in a destructive manner. Bobby was not allowed matches or sharp instruments because of his history.

Near the end of November just before the Thanksgiving holiday, Bobby came into the treatment area and plopped down on a beanbag chair. "You seem kind of distracted," I said. He hadn't said anything to me as we walked down the hall together, either. Usually, he told me about school. He had even confessed that he was ten years old but was only in second grade because he missed so much school due to operations on the burns.

"No, I'm not distracted. I want to invite you to come visit me after Christmas," he said.

"OK. So, do you want me to come to your house?"

"No. I'll be in the hospital, like I am every Christmas vacation."

"Which hospital?" I sat down in a small chair by the table we used for drawing and handwriting.

"Every Christmas I go to Mary Bridge Children's for another skin graft. This time, it's going to be on my right leg."

"Well, just tell me when I should visit, and I'll be there."

He looked at me as though to say, "Sure, that's what you say, but you won't show up."

We continued the session, and at the end, I told him to let me know when he wanted me to visit him in the hospital, and I would. At the next appointment, Bobby gave me the surgery date in December just after Christmas. He would be ready for a visitor on December 29th. He wanted me to come at ten o'clock in the morning.

For the next several sessions, he never mentioned his upcoming surgery or his desire for a hospital visit. I told him that he was making good progress with everything we planned to do, and I thought our therapy sessions would probably be finished by Easter. He did not respond.

Since we began treating the children from the reservation, I have been carrying the contract back and forth between the hospital administrator and the tribal council office. The office was on my way home if I took a certain route. We still lacked a signed contract, but the hospital administration continued our work with the children. Fran was about to discharge her patient, but I felt that Bobby needed more therapy after the Christmas holiday. The hospital administrator told me to do what I thought was needed for this youngster.

On the Saturday after Christmas, I went to Mary Bridge Children's Hospital to see Bobby. As soon as I walked into his room, he pushed the call button. He sat up in bed. When the nurse came into the room, he ordered, "Get my friend a better chair and bring her some coffee. Black, no sugar."

The nurse smiled. "OK, right away." She quickly left the room and returned with an upholstered chair, which she placed near his bed. She went out again and returned with a cup of coffee, black, no sugar in a ceramic mug. No paper cup for this guest. Evidently, she had done this before.

"So, how are you doing?" I asked.

"Oh, I'm getting along OK," Bobby said. "They will do another operation on my leg in the morning." I noticed there was already one bandage on his arm. He saw me looking at that and added, "Another skin graft."

"Oh," I replied. I learned not to ask too many questions early on in our relationship, or Bobby would just shut down completely. He would tell me things when he felt comfortable enough to do so. I told him about seeing the movie, "On Golden Pond" with my sister the day after Christmas. "You wouldn't like that movie," I said. "But the scenery in it was beautiful. It was on a lake in Massachusetts." I could see he was getting tired, so I left soon.

I returned the coffee cup to the nurse's station. "He's quite a guy," I said.

"Yes," the nurse behind the desk replied. "He's been here so often, sometimes I think of him as part of the staff. And we always do what he says, especially when he has company, which, frankly, is hardly ever." I was glad I went to see him because I knew he thought I would not. It was my way of letting him know he was worth something to me, at least.

I kept taking the new contract additions with me as I left the children's clinic and dropped them off at the tribal office on my way home. Sometimes I would get a call in the evening to tell me to pick up the contract on my way to work and deliver it to the hospital administration office. Later I learned that the contract had to go through the Tribal Administration Office, the Bureau of Indian Affairs, and the Public Health Department of the U.S. government each time even a comma changed.

As Easter came near, I knew that Bobby had made sufficient progress in therapy to be discharged. When I told him that we were just about done working together, he got very serious. "That means I won't be coming anymore. I won't see you anymore."

"That's about it," I said. "But you are doing great, and your school grades are good. You can dress yourself without help. I think you should be proud of the work you have done." Bobby turned away from me.

"Can I do the scooter board and swing again?" Bobby asked.

He knocked down blocks with more violence than I had ever seen from him before. He also threw the beanbags harder when he was in the hammock swing.

"I know you are angry, Bobby," I said in a soft voice. "But discharging you from therapy is a good thing." I tried to be reassuring. Bobby did not arrive for his last appointment. The school called to say he was sick and couldn't be at therapy. I never saw him again.

I had one more trip to the tribal office after Bobby was discharged. It was the end of April. The assistant administrator from the hospital and I drove to the reservation. In the meeting room, several members of the tribe waited for us. We sat down with them and the officer from the U. S. Public Health Department. After all the introductions, the contract was signed by all tribal members present, the assistant administrator from the hospital, and the officer from the U.S. Public Health Department. I was the only non-signer of the contract at the table. Not being one to keep my mouth shut, when the signing was finished and most of the people had left, I said to the chief, "I had no idea this was so involved. I would probably kill myself if things I needed to do took so long."

He looked directly into my eyes and without expression said, "Many of us do."

I felt terrible. I had been tactless. I had known other American Indians, but only then did I become aware of how complicated and difficult treaties made their lives. It was a lesson in humility that I would need later in my career with other Indigenous peoples and one I have never forgotten.

Chapter 8

Francis Haddon Morgan Center

In September 1985, I left the Children's Therapy Unit to work at the Francis Haddon Morgan Center in Bremerton, Washington. The Center was started in 1982 by a child psychologist who was particularly interested in children with autism, or autistic-like tendencies. The youngsters treated there lived on the campus in eight cottages. There was a school as well as a gym, a group center, and administrative offices.

Autism was not a diagnosis that we often heard in the late 1970s and early 1980s. The disorder was difficult to accurately diagnose and was considered a psychiatric disorder, not a neurological disorder. Emotional problems were not associated with brain function or genetics during that time. The understanding of genetics, development, and brain function impacting behavior was in its infancy. Brain research using Computer Tomography (CT) scans and Magnetic Resonance Imaging (MRI) and functional Magnetic Resonance Imaging (fMRI) was relatively new. With my background in sensory-motor/sensory integration theory and treatment, I was employed to use my understanding of those theories as well as my OT knowledge in treating the whole person.

The clients at the Center ranged in age from four to twenty-one. The children were required to walk to and from the group cottages to the school and gym areas. The founder of the center believed in routines and structure as well as skill training. The clients would eventually need to live more independently. Dr. Morgan was beginning to embrace the use of sensory stimulation and changes in the environment to accompany routines and psychological theories. Some of the residents had multiple diagnoses, such as cerebral palsy or Tourette's syndrome. Tourette's syndrome is characterized by twinges of movement, repetitive verbal expressions, or arm flailing in an uncontrollable manner.

One of the things I most wanted for the younger children at the Center was a more normal childhood experience. When I began working there, I asked my supervisor if the children ever went around the neighborhood to trick or treat.

"No. We never have done that in the four years I've been here. Do you think it's important? What if they get scared?"

"I do think it's important. After all, they're kids, and I believe they're entitled to the same experiences as every other child, especially at Halloween."

"Well, I suppose we could try it. You are here until eight. If we went after supper, you could go along." We decided to walk the younger children around the neighborhood. We would let them wear capes, baseball hats, and jeans. No fancy costumes or masks. We worked on saying "trick or treat" because many of the children did not talk much if at all. We practiced how to hold out a bag for treats. The aides from the younger children's residence halls would go along to help. The teenagers were already planning a Halloween party at their residence so they would not be walking around the neighborhood.

It was dark by the time we left the facility to walk into the neighborhood. The children held grocery bags, although a couple of children did not want to carry their bags, so the aides held those bags for them. At the first house, we stood in a bunch. The homeowner seemed a bit overwhelmed by the fifteen children and six adults at his door.

Before we went to the second house, I suggested that each aide take two or three children, and we would all go to separate houses. We would cover opposite sides of the street. I walked with Brenda and only one other child. At first, Brenda, who was a non-verbal, thin, six-year-old, would not knock on a door or ring a doorbell, so the other child and I did that. After the third house, Brenda was all smiles. The other youngster could say, "Trick or treat." At one house, the homeowner said he had never seen these children before. "They live up the street," I said.

"Oh, are these kids from that institution?"

"Yes. We thought they should have a fun night just like other kids," I replied. (This was before the HIPAA privacy legislation was in effect. Also, these children were not considered patients, only children in training.)

"That's great!" He gave my kids some extra candy.

We traveled three blocks and then headed back to the residence halls. All the children smiled. They seemed a bit excited, so we walked around the grounds at the Center for fifteen minutes before going inside to calm down before bedtime. The residential aides monitored the distribution of candy over the next few weeks to decrease sugar overload.

One of my other ideas directed the older residents to cook Thanksgiving dinner on the Saturday before Thanksgiving. We invited their parents to come for an evening together. Most of the children's parents visited twice a month, but there were several children who had no family visitors. Most of the older clients, ages fifteen and older, had never been home with their families for the holiday since moving into the Center.

We wrote and mailed invitations to all the families of the older residents. We also invited the Director of the Center and his wife with a written invitation. One of the teenage clients was skilled in drawing, so he decorated all twenty invitations.

We began working on cooking skills using real pots and pans. Many of the older residents were used to making pizza or heating frozen dinners on Sunday night, but few of them had ever peeled a potato, opened a can, baked a pie, or roasted a turkey. Two of the aides and three clients took the van and went grocery shopping after school one day. They bought everything we needed for the dinner. I did not live on the campus, but because my hours were from 11 a.m. to 8 p.m. on Tuesday through Saturday, I was present for all the preparations and much of the cleanup. All of this was exciting and created a great deal of anticipation.

I helped them bake pies three days before the dinner. We put them into a large cupboard for safekeeping. The cupboard had a padlock just in case someone decided to try the pie before dinner. The day before the dinner, we assembled green bean casseroles, peeled potatoes for mashing, and stuffed turkeys, which we put in the refrigerator.

The morning of the dinner, the aides put the turkeys into the ovens, and when I got to work at 11 a.m., we began setting tables, decorating the large room, and cooking the rest of the meal. Parents began arriving at five p.m. Two boys who we thought might have a meltdown in a large group were assigned to hanging up coats. That task kept them in the hallway until the actual dinner. One resident who was more verbal served light snacks while others helped two aides and me in the kitchen. We mashed potatoes, made gravy, and sliced the turkeys.

Everyone seemed to enjoy themselves. Clients who could talk chatted with family members. Residents who were non-verbal also sat with family or staff. They smiled a lot and nodded their heads. We did not have outbursts, meltdowns, or incidents during the whole evening. The parents left at nine. They thanked the Director and their youngsters.

I helped clean up, then headed home to Tacoma. I was exhausted but grateful that everything went so well. When I returned to work on Tuesday, the Director called me into his office. "That was a great evening," he said.

"Thank you. I thought it went well."

"My wife came away with an entirely different idea of the capabilities of these residents. She always thought they couldn't learn anything. Maybe I'd given her that impression, but she was delighted to see how well they did in a social situation. She was thrilled with the food, too. We're going to do this again next year."

"That sounds wonderful." I was excited by the success. I knew the kids worked hard and learned to cook something besides pizza. "I hope that the residents will receive some thank-you notes from their parents. They worked hard to put everything together for a great night."

"I will suggest that when I get in touch with a couple of the parents. Some of them called to thank me, but I think they need to thank their kids, too." I left his office feeling gratified.

Right after Christmas, Anita, a nurse in one of the younger children's residence halls, asked if I would go with her to Lucy's doctor's appointment.

"What seems to be the problem with Lucy?" I asked. "Isn't she the little blond, curly-haired kindergartener?"

"Yes. She is having trouble walking, and we have an appointment with an orthopedic surgeon. She's the one with mild cerebral palsy, too. You know that if a child is not ambulatory, she can't stay here," she reminded me.

"I'm sure I can arrange to go with you. What time?"

"We need to leave here at 1:30. I'll drive. The van will transport her, because we can't take kids in our own cars, you know."

"OK. I'll be in the employee parking lot at 1:15 and ride with you." I let my supervisor know that I would be off campus in the afternoon for Lucy's appointment. He agreed that it would be good for me to go along. There was no staff physical therapist, so I was the best option for helping with this orthopedic appointment. I had only worked with Lucy in class and had never had her on my individual treatment schedule.

When we arrived at the orthopedic doctor's office, the nurse filled out the paperwork, and I sat with Lucy. She did not speak much, but she liked looking at magazine pictures in the reception area. Her medical diagnosis was both cerebral palsy (CP) and autism.

The nurse called us into the examination room. Anita lifted Lucy up onto the exam table just before the doctor walked in. He performed the usual examination routine, which is often done by nurses now. He checked her pulse and heart, looked at her eyes, ears, and nose. He asked what the problem was, and Anita told him Lucy would not walk to school down the hill. She did not walk much in the residence hall, either. She complained about painful feet when she walked.

"She probably just wants you to do things for her," he said.

"She's not like that. She enjoys school, and she plays with other children in the play area. It's just within the past few months that she doesn't want to walk," Anita said.

At this point, the doctor had not even removed Lucy's shoes and socks to look at her feet. I took off her shoes and socks, hoping he would examine Lucy's feet. He picked up one of her feet and glanced at it while continuing to talk with Anita.

"Well, there's nothing I can do," he said.

"Excuse me," I said. "Aren't you even going to watch her walk?"

"Oh, well yes, I guess I had better do that," he responded.

I put Lucy down on the floor and asked Anita to walk over to the door. "Go walk to Nurse Anita," I coaxed her.

Lucy began to walk. Her face tensed up, and her hands began to flap, then she fisted them. When she nearly fell, the doctor picked her up and put her back on the exam table. He began looking more carefully at her feet. Even Anita and I could see that the muscles in her arches had shortened, pulling her feet into an odd angle.

"We can't take care of her at the hospital," the doctor said. "If you can guarantee she will have twenty-four-hour nursing care at the residence hall, I will operate and stretch these muscles. But you need to provide her care. We do not have the capacity to help a child like this in our hospital.

"We can provide the treatment she needs after surgery," Anita assured him. "When can we schedule the surgery?"

"Early next week. I'll tell my secretary to get her in on Tuesday. Early in the morning around seven."

"Great. Thank you," Anita said, smiling at him.

"Thank you," I said, although I did not smile.

We left the exam room after replacing the socks and shoes on Lucy's feet. The driver was waiting to take her back to the Center. Anita and I got into her car. As soon as the door was shut, Anita said, "Thank you for coming with me. I don't think I would have pushed that doctor to watch Lucy walk if you hadn't been with me. I'm not sure if I even would have taken off her shoes and socks, to tell you the truth."

"Oh, sure you would have, but it's always nice to have some backup," I said.

Lucy's surgery went well. The nursing staff carefully followed the after-care instructions. Bandages were changed regularly, and Lucy got to ride in a wagon to and from school for the six weeks as she recovered. A physical therapist was hired on a short-term basis for her rehabilitation. With that dedicated attention, Lucy was walking to and from the classroom and around the grounds by the end of February.

To everyone's surprise, I turned in my resignation. I announced I was moving to Alaska to work in an Early Intervention Program in Anchorage by mid-March. I was glad that Lucy did not have to move to a nursing facility now that she could walk without pain again.

Shortly before I left the Francis Haddon Morgan Center, a team from the University of Washington Medical Center came to the campus to examine all the children. Medicine had advanced. Diagnoses were now more detailed and specific. Several children were diagnosed with genetic disorders other than autism. Some of the children with autism diagnoses had that diagnosis confirmed. A few changes were made in treatment where new medications were available. I was not available for the examinations but heard of the new diagnosis of Fetal Alcohol Syndrome for some of the residents.

Although I thought The Francis Haddon Morgan Center did a good job helping their residents, I was sure that children with these disabilities needed to be with their families. Help should be provided to the family as a whole. I also thought that children with disabilities should not be isolated. They should be helped to adapt to the general population and the general population, needed to be more accepting of persons with disabilities. The Francis Haddon Morgan Center was closed several years after I left, primarily due to funding shortages.

Chapter 9

Continuing Education Credits

In 1984, the state of Washington passed legislation requiring all Occupational Therapists, Physical Therapists and Speech Therapists to acquire a state license. We also needed continuing education credits to keep our license renewed. I decided to take a course at the University of Washington evaluating infants and young children that would count for those credits. Since most of the children I had worked with for the past several years were older, I felt I needed to know more about the evaluation process for infants and preschool-aged children.

In the Fall of 1985, the Elks Clubs of Washington state sponsored the course at the University of Washington in Testing the Young Child. The Elks Clubs had been providing funds for services to children throughout the state for many years. My father was an Elk, and I was familiar with the work of the service club.

Since working at Francis Haddon Morgan Center, my formal testing skills have been getting rusty. Most of the children on the autism spectrum did not submit well to formal testing. At the Morgan Center most of the evaluations were based on clinical observations and observing the children in their environment. Fortunately, that has since changed, and there are standardized tests that can be used with children suspected of being on the autism spectrum.

I kept in contact with the therapists at the children's clinic where I worked before changing jobs. One of the physical therapists, Cindy, and I could meet in Fife and drive up to Seattle together. Since the class was taught all day on Monday, I did not need to take any time off from work, because I worked Tuesday through Saturday. The course lasted nearly three months. We completed a full twelve sessions and finished just before Christmas, 1985. Fritz was in school, and I did not have to think about a sitter for him.

When Cindy and I arrived the first day at the university, all the therapists taking the course were in a lecture room. We introduced ourselves, talked about where we worked and the diagnoses of children we treated. We were each assigned a mentor who was either on the faculty or a graduate student. My mentor was a graduate student who was completing her master's degree in occupational therapy that fall semester. She was at least twenty years my junior, had no children of her own, and had minimal clinical experience. She moved directly from her undergraduate degree to graduate school. Marlene had only done a thirteen-week clinical affiliation in pediatrics. Her plan was to teach in an occupational therapy program when she finished the master's degree. Marlene planned to go on for a doctorate, too. She was well-versed in the testing procedures, however, and that was what I came for.

For the first three children I was assigned to test, I used the Bayley Scales of Infant Development, a system that was designed to test babies and very young children for motor development. Although I had not worked with many youngsters that age, all the testing went well, and my mentor's feedback was mostly positive. Joey, the next child I was assigned was a four-year-old. I was to use the Peabody Developmental Motor Scales, which test for both fine motor and gross motor development.

Joey clung to his mother when I approached them in the waiting area. I asked his mother to join us in the testing room.

Once seated, I began the fine motor part of the test, and Joey always looked toward his mother before responding to my instructions. He seemed anxious about making a mistake and looked for his mother to nod her head when he selected the correct answer. I decided to ask his mother to leave the room because I felt Joey was not responding for himself. When his mother went into an observation area, Joey was still reluctant to give an answer. When the scheduled test time was over, accurate responses were minimal. My mentor was not pleased. We scheduled Joey for a repeat test the following Monday.

On our next testing time, Marlene sat with the mother in the observation room. When she saw that I still was getting little cooperation, she entered the room and tried to test Joey herself to show me how it should be done. He was even less cooperative with her. I suggested that we move on to the gross motor portion of the test, which included things such as running, hopping, skipping, and walking a balance beam. We moved to the larger treatment area. Marlene excused herself to attend a meeting.

The mother stood to the side of the room while I asked Joey to perform the large body movements. He complied well with these tasks, and I was able to score that portion of the test. The testing ended on a happy note for both the mother and child.

Once a month we met with the referring physicians. We all sat together in a large conference room. When it came time for me to present my results for this anxious youngster, I explained that I felt Joey was so anxious about making a mistake that the fine motor portion of the Peabody Developmental Motor Scales had invalid scores. Despite that, however, I was sure he would benefit from therapy even if it was just to gain confidence in himself away from his mother. Marlene was not on board for this recommendation. The discussion that ensued between my mentor and myself became tense. She demanded to know the basis for my recommendation. "In my experience, a child with this apparent anxiety needs to be able to rely upon his own judgement. He will not have his mother at his side during school hours, and he needs to work on his own."

"Your 'experience' does not replace valid test scores," Marlene said. "We are here to use the information from testing."

I decided not to respond. One of the physicians chimed in, "I think we should have Joey tested by our psychologist and see what she thinks. I'm willing to write a script for him to be treated by OT while we await the results of further testing. I know it'll be several weeks before the psychologist can test him. She's got a long waiting list. What do you think?" He looked around the room. Marlene did not say anything more. Most of the others in the room nodded their heads in agreement with the physician's decision, and we moved on to the next case.

I finished the course at the University of Washington with a passing grade, thanks to other mentors who argued my case with Marlene. I was glad to be done with the course.

Chapter 10

Move to Alaska

I was restless. Just before finishing the course at the University of Washington, I began to feel I needed to see some other area of the country or world. My son would be turning 19 and move on to a university, or maybe he would leave home to find a job soon. I did not want to live in Tacoma the rest of my life and began exploring other places that needed occupational therapists.

I saw a job advertisement for the Early Intervention Program in Anchorage, AK. Since I was just finishing the course at the University of Washington in testing infants and young children, I applied for that position. I asked Fritz if he wanted to move to Alaska, and he replied, "Heck, no, Mom. I want to stay here with my friends, but you can go."

Fritz and I were in Alaska in December 1970 to visit my first husband's father and stepmother. They lived in Juneau. Even though it was deep winter, the place was beautiful! We took the ferry from Seattle up through the Straits of Juan de Fuca into the Pacific Ocean, then to the Inside Passage through Canadian waters to Ketchikan, Alaska, then on to Juneau. In Juneau my father-in-law drove us to the edge of the snowcapped Mendenhall Glacier. At that time the glacier was all the way down to the road. There were only fifty-five miles of road around Juneau, and the weather was cold. Fritz was only four then, but that trip didn't seem long ago. Since I do not like hot weather, I knew that Alaska would be a good place for me to live at least for a while.

In January 1986, I had a telephone interview with the director of the Early Intervention Center in Anchorage. After I answered all her questions, she said she would hire me. Her next statement was, "You need to be here to begin work the first of March." I told her I would try to make that, but part of that would depend on my having a place to live. She said, "That's your problem."

A friend at church whose son, David, lived in Anchorage. He rented rooms out at his home. David was a Medical Evacuation (MedEvac) pilot and never knew when he would be flying out to some village to pick up a patient and fly back to Anchorage or take the patient all the way to Seattle. I told her about my dilemma, and she said she would talk to David. A couple of days later, David called me. After we talked for a while David said he would rent a room to me.

Next, I focused on Tacoma. Fritz and I talked about renting rooms to a couple of students at the University of Puget Sound, which was just two blocks from our house. In the past we rented a room to students a couple of times before, so he had some landlord experience. Fritz had a community college friend who wanted to live in Tacoma, so he immediately acquired one renter. Before I left for Anchorage, we found a UPS student to rent another room, too. With that handled, I booked my flight to Anchorage for the last week of February. I made arrangements for my car to be shipped to Anchorage on the ferry and called David to let him know when I would arrive in Anchorage so he could pick me up at the airport. Soon I was off to have my adventure.

I stayed at the Early Intervention Center for only six months. During that time, I flew with several other therapists to Ketchikan to evaluate children. We spent a week doing the evaluations and making recommendations. Three of the children came with their mothers from an island reservation just west of Ketchikan. There was no occupational therapist in Ketchikan, but one therapist came up from Seattle to treat children once a month. At that time there was no school of Occupational Therapy in Alaska and only five or six OTs in the whole state besides the two of us that worked for the Early Intervention Center in Anchorage.

While I worked at the Early Intervention Center, I drove to the homes of the children. Then once a month the child was brought to the Center by a parent, and the child was seen by the entire team, which included a Physical Therapist, Occupational Therapist, Speech Therapist and Early Childhood Educator. At the team meeting children were reassessed by clinical observations. The team would decide what needed to be changed in the treatment plan.

One of the homes I went to was a quarter mile out in the woods. I drove to a place where I could park my car safely. Then I would hoist my bag with therapy things in it over my shoulder and hike the quarter mile through the forest and across a creek to the single room log cabin where the family lived. Only one child lived there. Since the room was small, often the parents would lie on the bed while I worked on the floor near the wood stove to work with the child. He was only six months old and had Down syndrome. He was just learning to roll over and lift his head up to look around.

David did not like my descriptions of these home visits. In August, with winter fast approaching, David and I talked about changing to a job where I only had one place to work. He thought I would be safer if I drove only in Anchorage. His mother had told him to watch out for me, which I didn't know until much later. My car was not the best vehicle to own. It did have four-wheel drive, but it had problems more often than I thought it would. I had to replace the battery, change spark plugs and do a couple of other things when it broke down. I became a regular customer at a garage David sent me to.

Several of the therapists at the early intervention center were young women who planned to work through the summer and then return to the Lower 48. Two of the early childhood special education teachers were going to work at school districts, one was moving to Juneau, and the other was going to Fairbanks. I decided that if I could find a different job in Anchorage, I would leave the Early Intervention Center in the fall.

I found a large nursing facility in Anchorage run by the Sisters of Providence. They needed an occupational therapist. The Sisters of Providence owned the largest hospital in Anchorage and was also starting an outpatient facility to treat both adults and children. The nuns wanted to be able to help patients from the time they entered the hospital through their recovery and then returning home. I applied for the job.

Chapter 11

Our Lady of Compassion Nursing Facility

In late September 1986, I interviewed at Our Lady of Compassion Nursing Facility. Their full-time OT was leaving in November as her husband was in the Air Force and he would soon move to another base. The other OT was a woman a bit younger than myself who worked on call, or part-time depending on what the facility needed. She was married with three children. Her husband was often away, as he was a pilot and an engineer.

Although I had never worked in a nursing home at this point in my career, I was a good candidate for this job. Twelve pediatric patients in the facility needed OT. I had never worked with patients in an extended care facility, but I had supervised students who were studying occupational therapy, and I had worked with one student in a school district who was Native American. I was introduced to quite a few Alaska Natives who didn't speak English in the nursing home, but there were two interpreters who also worked in the facility who spoke the languages of those patients.

During my interview, the Director of therapy noticed that I often changed jobs. "I would like to hire you, but you will have to commit to working here for at least two full years. If you would be willing to do that, the job is yours."

"I will agree to work for two years, but I do have plans to be in Washington over the Christmas holiday. I need to keep that commitment. I can begin the first of October, then take the two weeks off in December and be back just before January 1st, if that's OK with you."

The administrator agreed to that plan, and we shook hands. Then she escorted me around to meet other therapists in the facility. I met one physical therapist who had worked there for several years and one speech therapist besides the two occupational therapists.

When I told David that evening that I would be working at Our Lady of Compassion Nursing Facility, he was glad I would not be driving around for my job anymore. He really liked that I would no longer be hiking to remote cabins during the winter months.

Since I committed to be in Anchorage for another two years, David suggested I find myself an apartment. After all, I was only supposed to live at his house for two months when I got there in March. I agreed. I needed a place of my own.

Chapter 12

Getting Some Children to School

When I began working for the nursing facility, I realized that five children were supposed to be attending school, and they were not. I told my supervisor that the federal government required children ages three years old and above to attend school even if they had special needs. She said she would bring that up with the administration and the pediatrician. The following afternoon, I saw the pediatrician in the hall and told him that several children needed to be attending school.

"These kids won't learn anything in school. They are all mentally retarded or brain damaged," he said.

"That doesn't make any difference. The law does not discriminate based on intelligence. Also, the kids need better wheelchairs since they will be going to school." I was adamant.

"What about Pumpkin Head?" he asked. "Pumpkin Head" was what he called Judy, one little girl who was five years old and had a very large head. She was born with hydrocephalus, which is swelling of the brain by fluid retention. Little Judy had difficulty holding her head up because it was so large. It was difficult for her to sit upright, also.

"Yes, especially Judy," I replied. "We need a special wheelchair to help keep her upright, but she needs to be in school, too. It's the law."

After the facility administrator learned of the federal legislation, I was given the opportunity to contact the Anchorage School District Department of Special Education regarding the children. Both the physical therapist and occupational therapist from the schools came to assess the children. They also helped me order the proper wheelchair for each child. By the middle of November those children were attending school in special education classrooms. The school bus arrived at eight in the morning to take them to school and brought them back to the nursing facility by two thirty in the afternoon. The nursing staff mentioned to me how much happier those children seemed to be. They slept better at night and ate better, too. When they were allowed to sit in the hall on the weekends, they often smiled at people passing by, which they had not done much before they started school.

I was glad that even Judy, who was still referred to as "Pumpkin Head" by the pediatrician, seemed more attentive when I worked with her. It was as though what I said to her meant something, and she would try to follow my instructions as we worked on movements of her arms and head. It pleased me and the nursing staff that the children were doing so well with going to school.

Chapter 13

Yupik Patient

One afternoon Martha, my supervisor, came to me with a request. She said there was no order to work with one of the Yupik patients, but the nursing staff was very concerned about an elderly woman who had Diabetes and a heart condition. The patient was not eating well and refused to leave her room to go to the dining room or get any exercise by walking in the halls. The interpreter was not having any luck talking with the woman about what she needed to do either. I said I'd give it a try but could not promise any more success than anyone else.

I approached George, the interpreter, and asked what the woman was saying to him. He said that Mrs. Yaari wanted to make herself a new kuspuk. A kuspuk is a garment that women wear when the weather gets a bit warmer. We went to Room 304, where Mrs. Yaari was. When I knocked on the door, she said, "Go away." Then George knocked on the door, and Mrs. Yaari said, "Come in." I wondered how she could tell the difference in our knocking on her door. She was also speaking English!

George introduced me and told her that I would buy her some material to make a kuspuk, but I needed to know what color she liked, and if she needed rickrack of different colors. I also wanted to know how much material and rickrack she needed. Would she need needles and thread, too? I asked George if she wanted to use the sewing machine in the occupational therapy department. George asked her that, and she pointed her finger at me and laughed. Then she said something to George.

"What did she say?" I asked.

"I'll tell you when we get in the hall." We left the room.

"She was laughing about the sewing machine. She hates white people because she thinks they are stupid. You just proved her right. None of the older women from Bethel would ever use a sewing machine. They sew everything by hand." George told me.

"Oh, I guess I gave her a good laugh. Well, I'll stop by JoAnne's Fabrics after work and purchase her supplies. I know the manager because I work there in the evening sometimes. That job helped me stay awake when it got dark at three thirty in the afternoon this winter. "

At the fabric store I consulted with the manager about fabric and rickrack for the kuspuk. I bought some beautiful yellow cloth with delicate green flowers in the pattern. I selected two shades of green rickrack, also.

"You'll have to stop by Fred Meyer's to get some paraffin," the store manager told me.

"What's that for?"

"These old Eskimo women always cover the thread with beeswax or paraffin. This keeps the thread from twisting and knotting up. It also sort of waterproofs it as well. We're out of beeswax here right now."

I thanked her and left. When I had everything gathered together, I took it to work with me the following day. "George, are you busy? I want to take the fabric and other things to the lady in Room 304."

"OK, I'll go with you. I can't stay long, though."

We went to Mrs. Yaari's room, and I handed her the bag with everything in it. She checked the items out, then looked at us and waved her hand to shoo us out of her room. George and I left. I thought perhaps that the patient would at least say, "Thank you," but she did not.

The following week I happened to walk past Room 304. The door was open, and I looked in. Mrs. Yaari was tearing the material apart. I was upset, so I stopped at the other translator's desk to let her know what I had seen.

"Oh, no, don't worry about that. That's how these older women measure and cut their project. From the middle of your neck to the end of your arm is how long the body of the kuspuk needs to be. It will fall from your shoulder to just below your hip joint," she told me. They don't use measuring tapes or scissors to measure and cut anything."

I did not walk past that door again. Then a couple of weeks later I was standing at the nurse's station talking with the nurse about another patient. When we were done, the nurse said, "Oh, I wanted to thank you for your help with Mrs. Yaari. The patient is in Room 304. She is eating in the dining room now and also walking around the halls. She even stops to chat with another woman from Bethel who sits in the lounge sometimes. She's quite a changed patient. She loves showing off her new kuspuk."

"Oh, I'm glad I was able to help." I turned to walk away and just about stumbled over an older woman who was standing near me. The nurse said, "Don't you recognize her?"

I looked at the woman more closely and realized it was Mrs. Yaari from Room 304. She was standing there in her new kuspuk. She was even smiling! I smiled back and returned to the OT department, happy to know that even without a doctor's order, I was able to help make a positive change in someone's life.

Chapter 14

Child Patient

At the end of January Katie Smith arrived in the pediatric section of the nursing home. She had been abused by her parents, who were both from the Lower 48. Katie was now a ward of the state of Alaska. Although she was three years old, she did not speak and was not able to sit up or hold her head up because of the brain damage she had suffered. After I evaluated her, I asked to treat her three times a week for one hour per session. The pediatrician and the state agreed, and I got the prescription from the pediatric neurologist to work with her on my suggested schedule.

When I first worked with Katie, she would stiffen her whole body if I moved her too fast during our exercises. I quickly learned to move her very slowly, and I shared that with the nursing staff so they would also move her slowly when they changed her diaper or rolled her over in the crib. After I worked with her on head control for nearly six weeks, she was able to turn herself over from her back to her stomach and lift her head slightly off the mat. Katie was making progress, but I did not know how much more progress she would make, as she still had a shunt to drain excess fluid off her brain.

One afternoon Martha, my supervisor, called me into her office. "I'd like you to meet Mr. McKinney from the District Attorney's office. He has something for you," Martha said. I took the envelope from Mr. McKinneyand opened it. Quickly scanning the letter, it stated that I was being called as an expert witness to testify in the trial against Katie's parents. If found guilty of beating Katie, she would be in permanent custody of the State of Alaska. The trial was set for April.

"I haven't worked with her very long. I don't know what kind of progress she'll make between now and April."

"What's on trial is how much damage has been done and what the prognosis is for her potential. This is a criminal abuse case and custody hearing," Mr. McKinney stated.

"Have you ever testified in court before?" Martha asked.

"No. I gave a deposition once in an auto accident case, but that's all."

Mr. McKinney handed me his card and said, "If you have any questions, please call." He left the room.

I was in shock about this situation. I did not have a doctorate or even a master's degree in occupational therapy. Although I had learned some of the skills about working with children with cerebral palsy or brain damage while working at the clinic in Puyallup, I was not officially trained in Neurodevelopmental Treatment (NDT). I did not have a certificate in NDT. I felt inadequate.

I continued to work with Katie regularly. Although she did not talk, she was beginning to make a few sounds. I usually played soft classical music during our therapy sessions. She began to smile when I put a record on the phonograph, knowing there would be music while we worked together.

At the trial, I was told where to sit in the courtroom. My seat was directly behind Katie's parents and their lawyer. I could not see their faces, only the back of their heads. When I was called to the witness stand, the state attorney asked how long I had been working with Katie and what, if any, progress she had made. Then he asked what her problems were now. I explained that her movement patterns were more like a three-month-old baby's rather than a three-year-old child's. Also, she still overreacted to light touch and did not speak, nor did she feed herself.

His next question was, "In your opinion, what do you believe is her potential?"

I had to admit that I was only speculating; however, I believed that she probably would never walk or display good hand movements. She would never live independently, nor learn much even if she went to school. The defense attorney did not ask me any questions. I was dismissed. Next, the pediatric neurologist who treated Katie was called to the witness stand. He and I had not talked about Katie's parents' trial.

He was asked similar questions to the ones I was asked, and he basically corroborated what I said. I breathed a sigh of relief, feeling like he assessed Katie's potential the same as I had. When all the testimony was finished, the judge stated that the parents were guilty, and they would be sentenced to a minimum of five years in prison. Katie would be a ward of the state.

After the trial, I was able to see the parents as they were lead out of the courtroom. I had never looked at them while I was on the witness stand. Neither of them showed any facial expression. When I got back to the nursing facility, I told Martha the outcome of the trial. I also said that the pediatric neurologist had essentially backed up my testimony. I was grateful for his testimony. Martha said, "Why don't you go home? You've had quite an ordeal. I'll see you tomorrow." I left and went home to David's to change my clothes. After getting into jeans, a sweatshirt, and my heavy coat, I headed to Earthquake Park to walk off my remaining anxiety. I prayed that I would never have to testify in that kind of a case again. I never did.

Two months after the trial, Katie was adopted by a couple in Seattle. I met her adoptive parents during a brief visit and recommended that she be evaluated at the University of Washington and continue treatment there. They said that they would follow through on that recommendation and had already lined up a pediatrician who also taught at the University of Washington. Katie left Alaska two days later, with her new, loving family.

Chapter 15

The Soapstone Carver

In June, an Inuit native man from the Koyuk village on Norton Sound in northwest Alaska came into Our Lady of Compassion Care Center in the skilled-bed unit. He had suffered a severe stroke that caused him to lose motor function on his left side. He spent most of his time in bed even though he was conscious. He seemed unwilling to get up and participate in meals or do anything. He spoke little English, so Rita, the physical therapist, and I used one of our translators during our evaluations.

We learned that besides fishing and hunting, Mr. Amagoalik had been a long-time soapstone carver. He needed to rebuild his motor coordination and hand strength in order to carve again.

Through the interpreter, I asked Mr. Amagoalik if he would learn to get dressed and sit up in a wheelchair before we brought him some soapstone to carve. The Care Center required him to use the therapy room table to carve. He would not be able to carve in his room or in the dining room. It took a minute for him to understand what I needed him to do, then he told me, "Yes."

We began working on some upper-extremity exercises, both on his right and left sides. The physical therapist and I worked together with Mr. Amagoalik for two hours a week. He was quite willing to work with us. We made progress. We also learned that he wanted to return to his home in Koyuk.

After three weeks of therapy Mr. Amagoalik regained some movement in his left shoulder and elbow. I had been using hand weights on his right arm and hand to improve his strength. He was also willing to get dressed with the help of the nursing assistant. He began meeting other patients from Northwest Alaska, although none were from his village, by eating his meals in the dining room.

One afternoon I went to see Mr. Amagoalik with George, the interpreter. "Please ask him where I can get some soapstone," I told George. Mr. Amagoalik seemed surprised.

"You can probably get some at the Alaska Native Art store on Fourth Avenue in Anchorage," George told me after translating what Mr. Amagoalik had said.

"Please tell him I'll visit the store this weekend," I said. George translated what I had said and Mr. Amagoalik looked at me and smiled while shaking his head up and down.

On Saturday I went to the Alaska Native Art store and talked to a sales person. Sure enough he told me that I could get soapstone, but he needed to know what size. "Something not too big because it's for a patient of mine. His right-hand grip is pretty good, but he can barely move his left. I plan to assist by holding the stone myself, or the interpreter will help hold the stone."

The salesperson disappeared into the back room and returned with a piece of soapstone approximately six inches tall and three inches wide. It was not exactly rectangular, but it was narrower at the top than the bottom. "Will you need chisels and knives, too?" he asked.

"I don't think so. The nursing facility has some tools, but if there is anything else we need, can I get them from here?"

"Yes, we do have some carving tools here."

"What do I owe you?"

"Nothing," he replied. "Consider it a donation. It's not often we get a request like yours. We're glad to help. I would like a picture of the finished product when your patient is done with it though."

I thanked him and left.

When I showed Mr. Amagoalik the soapstone I had gotten, he smiled approvingly at me. "We can try it out this afternoon in the OT area," I told him. He seemed to understand.

I laid out some tools for him at a table. I thought he would be happy to have everything all set up. George was also present. When Mr. Amagoalik arrived with the nursing assistant pushing him in the wheelchair, he looked everything over and shook his head, "No". He told George that he wouldn't use any of the tools on the table, and that he needed an electric tool that spins around. George looked at me and said, "He needs a Dremel tool."

"What's that?" I asked. George explained that he had one at home that he could bring in tomorrow. I'll have to show you, it's hard to describe.

"Please tell Mr. Amagoalik that I'm sorry and that we'll try again tomorrow afternoon." I realized again how little I knew about the lives of the Native Americans who lived in Alaska.

George took our patient back to his room and I regretted that I had not asked the man at the Alaska Native Art store what kind of tool my patient would need to do his carving. Although maybe he would not have known either.

The following day George came in with Mr. Amagoalik and we positioned him at the table with the soapstone. The correct tool was plugged into the wall and ready to use. Mr. Amagoalik smiled at both of us as he picked up the Dremel tool with his right hand. It spun around like a drill. I held the soapstone on the left side and he began cutting the stone. He seemed to be able to see veins and spaces in the soapstone that

I could not. We worked for about forty-five minutes, finding the beginnings of a good outline. I had another patient to see before leaving for the day. George wheeled Mr. Amagoalik back to his room to get ready for dinner.

After a couple of weeks, the soapstone began to look like a penguin. I was surprised since there are no penguins in Alaska, or in the Northern Hemisphere at all, except maybe in a zoo. But maybe I shouldn't have been surprised. Arctic Circle native people have a long history of reverence for all land and sea animals.

"So are you making a penguin?" I asked, forgetting he spoke little English. He looked at me and smiled. "Yes, he said. "When I return to my village I will take this with me. Then there will be a penguin above the Arctic Circle." Then he laughed.

I laughed, too. I realized that Mr. Amagoalik spoke much more English than I had ever imagined and he had not wanted me to know that until now. He said he did not feel comfortable working with a woman by himself. He always wanted George with us. That was more consistent with his culture. In his village a man and a woman who were not his mother or wife did not work alone together. Learning about his comfort levels was an important cultural lesson for me.

About three weeks later, Martha called me into her office as I arrived at work. "You need to know that Mr. Amagoalik had another stroke last night and I'm sorry to say he did not survive. His body will be sent back to Koyuk for a customary Inuit ceremony."

"I'm so sorry. And shocked, too. I thought he was doing so well. Will the soapstone he was working on go to the village, too?"

"No. Since carving was part of his therapy, the soapstone is considered ours. It will probably go into our gift shop, or go to the Alaska Native Art store."

I bought the unfinished soapstone penguin myself from our gift shop and continue to display it in my home office to remember Mr. Amagoalik and what a wonderful man he was and what he taught me about the Inuit customs.

Chapter 16

Alaska Treatment Center

After my two years were over at Our Lady of Compassion Nursing Facility, I took a job at Alaska Treatment Center, an outpatient facility, owned by the Sisters of Providence. Their overall vision was to treat patients from the time they entered their hospital in Anchorage until the patient was well enough to return home. However, if the patient needed continued therapy, the Sisters of Providence could provide that as well.

With this job I still would not have to drive all over. It would also pay a bit better than the job at the nursing facility. My son, Fritz, was still in Tacoma and was about ready to finish community college. He did not know what he was going to do after he graduated, but he still had time to decide.

One weekend Fritz called to say, "What am I going to do, Mom? I'm about ready to be done with my two years of college."

"What do you want to do?" I asked.

"I don't know. I could be an accountant, I could get a degree in business administration, I suppose. I just can't seem to decide."

"Do you remember when we lived in Texas? When you were little, every evening when the Huntley and Brinkley newscast came on the TV, you would come into the family room and watch the whole show. You continued to do that even after we moved back to Washington. You would sit with Grandpa Court to watch that show during the week, too.

Think about that. Maybe you should consider getting a degree in TV or radio."

"Oh gosh. Washington State University has a great school of communication. It's the Edward R. Murrow School of Broadcasting. Maybe I should try getting into that."

We chatted some more and his whole voice sounded excited rather than depressed when we ended our conversation. I was happy that maybe he would follow through with that idea.

I liked working at the treatment center. My patients varied from adults to small children. There were several Alaska Natives on my caseload, too. They all spoke English and we got along well most of the time.

Chapter 17

Susie

In January 1989, I was working for the Alaska Treatment Center. One of the pediatricians referred a seven-year-old girl named Susie for occupational therapy. The referral said the child had eating problems. I assumed that Susie might have a cleft palate or chewing difficulties. When her mother brought her for the evaluation, I was surprised. I saw no physical problems. She talked without any difficulty. She smiled and chatted with me. She was petite for her age. Her dark hair was curly, and her dark eyes were quick to take in everything around her.

Her mother, Katie, told me that Susie often refused to eat. Sometimes she would go several days without eating. I soon realized that Susie used eating as a tool of control with her parents. Her "eating disorder" was psychological. Katie hovered over Susie while I was doing my evaluation. I suggested to Katie that Susie and I would be fine without her in the room, and that she should wait in the reception area while I finished the evaluation.

I tested Susie's response to tactile stimulation, both light pressure and deep pressure touch. I had her skip, hop, and jump as well as walk on the balance beam. She had no problems with any of that. I gave her the Fine Motor Tests of the Bruininks-Oseretsky Test of Motor Proficiency. She loved to draw, so I asked her to draw her favorite food. She drew a carrot. "It's like what bunnies eat," she told me.

"Oh, you like bunny food?" I asked.

"Yes. That's my favorite," she grinned.

After the evaluation, we went to the reception area. Katie was talking with the secretary. Susie took my hand. I leaned down and said that maybe she could come back next week. Then, straightening up, I turned to Katie and said I had to score the tests and write a report, but I would call to let her know what the results were and if I would recommend Susie for therapy. "Oh, I hope she did well for you," Katie said.

"She did just fine. We had fun. Didn't we, Susie?" She squeezed my hand and smiled at me.

When they left, Marsha, the secretary, told me that Katie had talked to her practically nonstop. She seemed extremely anxious about Susie doing well. Katie also confided that her husband was a fisherman and was often gone for extended periods of time. When he came home, Susie ate even less.

I called the referring physician and talked with him. "We might have a case of abuse on our hands," he said. "Be sure to check for signs of bruising, burning, or cutting. I want you to see her; I don't care what the OT test results are. For now, we are calling it a behavior disorder. Can you see her at least once a week?"

"Yes. I'll juggle some kids around and get her in after school," I said. "I assume she'll be seeing Laura, our child psychologist, too."

He assured me that Susie was scheduled for a full workup with Laura, but it would be awhile before she could get Susie in. I knew Laura was busy and wouldn't be able to see Susie for a month. The doctor told me he was referring Susie to social services as well, but they couldn't act until they had definite proof that Susie was being abused.

I rearranged my schedule, and the secretary made calls to parents about their new appointment times. Susie did have some slight problems with fine motor coordination, mostly with isolating finger movements. She also had a sensitivity to light touch, especially when I accidentally brushed against her. Susie would jump and run to a corner before she realized that my touch was unintended.

We began each therapy session with Susie running through an obstacle course, playing in the ball bath, then playing with playdough, or drawing pictures. We ended most sessions by playing "tea party" with real foods. I'm a pretty good actress, so I was the "princess." She was the "queen." Since she was the "queen," she could order me to eat or drink whatever I had put on the table. Usually, I placed a variety of foods on our little table. After I had eaten something and smacked my lips and rolled my eyes in delight, she would take a bite or a drink. We ended each session by eating nearly everything on the table – not just the sweet stuff, either.

When Laura was finished with her evaluation, she began seeing Katie once a week also. Since Katie had told Laura that she had a hard time getting Susie to therapy because she had to rely on neighbors to bring them in, Laura and I coordinated their treatment times. Katie lived beyond the city limits, and she did not have a car. Her husband always drove when he was home. He deliberately took the car keys with him when he was out fishing. Katie relied on neighbors to drive her everywhere she needed to go in the winter. In the summer, she and Susie walked a mile to the nearest bus stop just to go to the grocery store.

We had been seeing Susie for about six weeks when her father came into therapy. He wanted to know what we were doing with his daughter. I invited him to watch a session; however, I asked him please not to say anything. I would tell him the purpose of all the activities we were doing. To my surprise, he complied with my request. When Susie and I got to the end of the session and played "tea party," her father got up and walked over to the table. "Susie, you know you don't like cucumbers or peanut butter. Why, you don't even like carrots. I'll take that cookie. I'll be outside when you're done." He took both chocolate-chip cookies off the tray and walked out of the room.

Susie did not eat anything that day, no matter how much I smacked my lips. The following week Katie walked into our clinic with a black eye. She was wearing a cast on her left arm. "I fell and hit the coffee table," was her story. Her husband was fishing again and would be gone for six weeks.

During Susie's session, I saw several burn marks on her back when she was "diving" into the ball bath. As soon as they left, I called the physician, and he alerted social services. Laura and I talked about Susie that evening before we left the clinic. We did not know if she would return for therapy once social services got involved, or if she would be taken from her home.

Laura and I did not see Susie for a couple of weeks, then she returned to resume therapy with both of us. The social worker joined her first session to observe and to fill us in. Susie was taken from the home and was living with a foster family. Katie had filed a restraining order against her husband and was considering divorce. She was also in a safe home. The state decided that Laura and I would continue to work with Susie until Katie decided what she wanted to do. We were considered Susie's stable relationships at this point in her life.

Chapter 18

Orders to Move

I haven't mentioned much about my personal life. While in Anchorage, I maintained a vigorous outdoor life hiking and kayaking. In August of 1988, I spent a Sunday afternoon on a woodsy hike with Everett, who soon became my husband. Everett and I were both parishioners at the Episcopal church in Anchorage. We were introduced by mutual friends in August of 1988.

He was in the Air Force and had been in Alaska since 1985. We dated for three months before he asked me to marry him. We were married in the Episcopal church in January 1989. Then in March he was reassigned to Holloman Air Force Base in Alamogordo, New Mexico. Everett had to be on the base in Alamogordo by December 3rd. We began making plans for our travel to the Lower 48. I turned in my resignation immediately to allow time for the treatment center to find a replacement therapist for me. My final day was to be October 28, 1989. It never occurred to me that I would not be the only one leaving on that day. It turned out that Alaska Treatment Center closed at the end of October 1989.

On that last day, we therapists went out to lunch together. The lunch had been planned as a going-away celebration for me, but turned into a goodbye lunch for all of us. Since we only had a couple of patients scheduled in the afternoon, we took extra time to linger over lunch. All of us had been hired by other places by then. I had seen an ad for an OT position in a magazine and applied for a job with the Alamogordo School

District. After a phone interview, I was hired in their Special Education Department to begin in January 1990.

Laura and I had been seeing Susie since January. She was our last patient the day the clinic closed. I had told Susie a couple of weeks before that I was leaving. When we were done with our last session, I took her upstairs to Laura's office. Laura asked me to stay during their session. Since I had no other clients and had already packed up my desk, I said I could do that.

"How do you feel about Margret leaving us?" was one of the first questions Laura asked Susie.

"I hate her!" our little girl replied, folding her arms across her chest and pouting.

"So. What would you like to say to her/" Laura asked.

"I hate you! I don't want you to go."

"Well, I'm sorry," I said. "But I'm going to be moving away."

"You should stay here with me," Susie said. She rose from her chair, came over, and kicked me in the shin. Then her face turned from a scowl into one of extreme sadness, and tears began to roll down her cheeks.

I took her into my arms, and tears ran down my cheeks as well. I held her close, and we both cried. "I'll miss you very much. I'll always love you," I said.

I looked at Laura, who was nodding her approval. Our little girl regained her composure. It was time to go. The session was over. We walked her downstairs to join her foster mother. We hugged again. Susie and her foster mother left.

"That's the first time I've ever been abused by a patient," I said to Laura.

"She needed to get it out. That's why I asked you to be present. You both needed it," she said.

Laura was right. I needed to be in touch with the loss of my Alaska friends, the place itself, and the closing of the Alaska Treatment Center. I was able to keep in touch with some of the therapists for a while after we moved. I know one of our speech therapists moved to Fairbanks and married an engineer. Laura learned to fly and bought her own plane. None of us knew what happened to Susie and her mother. I prayed that Katie divorced her husband and went on to live a life free of that abusive relationship. And I hope Susie grew up strong and well.

Chapter 19

Above the Arctic Circle

The August before we left Alaska, I was approached by a nurse I had known at Good Samaritan Hospital in Puyallup, Washington. I was surprised to see Shelly. "Shelly, I thought you moved to Kotzebue."

"I did. I'm here in Anchorage to find some help. I'm looking for an OT who wouldn't mind coming up to Kotzebue over a weekend to do some evaluations and training at the nursing facility where I'm the manager and Director of Nursing and Rehab. Would you be interested?"

"Yes!" I said. "Can I bring my husband with me?"

"You can, but you'll have to pay for his flight up and back. I will have a room for you to stay in at my house, so you won't have to rent a room. Do you think you can fly up over Labor Day Weekend?"

"I'm sure we can. Do you want us there Friday afternoon? I'll work Saturday and Sunday then return to Anchorage on Monday."

"That's what I thought. Janet, one of the PTs you worked with at Good Samaritan Hospital will be coming to do the PT evals. You remember her, don't you?"

"Yes, I sure do. She conducted a weekend course on Inhibitive Casting for PTs in Alaska. Her workshop was hosted at Our Lady of Compassion Treatment Center when I was working there."

"I'll buy you the airline tickets for your flights and leave them at the airport. All you need to do is get there and jump on the plane."

Shelly and I shook hands and she was out the door. When I got home, I told Everett we were going to Kotzebue over Labor Day weekend. Kotzebue is a seaside town far North in Western Alaska. Some people say it almost touches Russia. The entire area holds less than 3,000 people, most of them Maniilaq Indians. Kotzebue is officially above the Arctic circle and has long, snowy and very cold winters. Summers are short.

Everett was a good sport about my new plans. I should have talked to him first before accepting the job. He did not object to my making those plans without talking to him first. "It will be fun to go and I'll take something to read while you're at work."

We left for Kotzebue on the Friday before Labor Day. Shelly picked us up at the airport and drove us to the nursing facility first just to show us around and introduce us to some of the staff. Then we went to her house where we met her foster child and her husband. She fixed dinner for us and we all talked for a bit before heading to bed.

The next morning, after a quick bite to eat, Shelly and I drove to the nursing home. On the way, Shelly explained that they were trying to turn eight beds into skilled beds so patients could be treated locally, Right now, patients were sent all the way to Anchorage.

"Some of those folks even have to go to Seattle! That's way too far away for family members to visit. We want to be able to keep our elderly patients here in Kotzebue near relatives and friends. We'd like them to either get therapy or die close to home. The Native people are close=knit and need family and friend connections. It is hard on everyone when a sick person is sent away and struggles alone."

Five patients waited to see me. I was introduced to two of them while they were at breakfast. The speech therapist and I worked together. Most of our evaluations were based on clinical observations. Translators assisted when needed. I wrote reports before the end of the day. On Sunday I saw three other patients. Again, I did clinical observations and quickly wrote up my reports.

I was impressed with one of the nursing assistants. Judy was very skilled and caring. I thought she would be a wonderful OT. I began talking to her about getting an OT degree, then coming back to her family in Kotzebue and working in the nursing home.

"I cannot leave town. If I did what you want, I would not be accepted when I returned," Judy told me.

I was startled. I could not believe what she was saying and continued to suggest that she become an occupational therapist. She began to avoid me.

I tried another route. I mentioned to Shelly that night that Judy would make an excellent occupational therapist.

"Oh, no. That doesn't work around here. Once you go away and try to come back, the people don't accept you. It's just their culture. That's what makes it so hard to send patients away, too."

"Oh goodness. I thought she was just not wanting to leave because it was too scary. Another fact about their customs I needed to understand."

Everett and I returned to Anchorage. The flight was nearly cancelled because of a storm blowing in from Russia. Fortunately, we got off the ground. It was a rocky flight, but we were home safe by the evening.

I flew back to Kotzebue three weeks later to follow up. With the assistance of the nursing staff following our instructions all five patients had made progress. They were all eating with the adaptive utensils we supplied. The three stroke patients had started to help themselves get dressed. They were eating in the dining room as well as participating in some activities. I wrote progress reports and then returned to Anchorage.

Shelly told me that the Health Department evaluated the PT, Speech Therapist and OT work. We made an impact. The Health Department was more than satisfied with our progress and authorized ten skilled beds in the facility, and two other beds that could be used either as skilled beds or regular patient beds. Shelly was thrilled and so was the community of Kotzebue. The entire town was happy that elderly and vulnerable patients could stay home to be treated. It was a relief that patients would not be flown out to Anchorage or Seattle.

With the Health Department approvals, Shelly lined up another OT. She was scheduled to come once a month for evaluations and to train aides. Regular scheduled occupational therapy was a significant progress.

Everett and I left Alaska at the end of October 1989 and headed to New Mexico where our new jobs were waiting.

Chapter 20

Alamogordo Public Schools

When we arrived in Alamogordo, New Mexico, I wanted to go directly to the school administration office, even before visiting the trailer park where we would live until we found a house.

So I walked into the school administration office, and stood in front of the secretary near the entrance. "Hi. I'm Margret Kingrey, the occupational therapist. Is Mrs. Verdin here? Is there any chance I can talk to her and let her know we've arrived?"

"Oh my. I've heard you were coming, but I didn't think you would be here so soon. I'll check to see if Mrs. Verdin is available." She picked up the phone and dialed. "Yes, Margret's here, standing right in front of me now."

The secretary put down the phone and said, "Mrs. Verdin will be right out. Her office is just across the hall." At that moment, a woman with graying hair and a lovely smile came from behind the door across the hall.

"Hi, I'm Bobby Verdin." She said as we shook hands. "Please call me Bobby. So glad to have you on board. Let's go into my office." We walked around to another hallway and, as she opened the door, she asked, "How was your trip down?"

"Good." I replied.

"Well, I have a couple of questions for you," she continued. "Can you see your way clear to begin working before the end of the year? If possible, could you start December 12?" We have several children waiting to be evaluated and I would appreciate getting them on the schedule before the holiday. If they need services, getting paperwork started this calendar year would help. It's partly a funding issue."

"I can start on Monday." I thought the less time I spent in the trailer, the better I would like it.

"The other thing is, you will be covering the Mescalero Apache Reservation School, which is about fifty miles from here. Do you have a problem with that?"

"No problem," I replied. "I don't have a car right now, but we will be going to Ruidoso on Saturday to visit the Subaru dealer. Hopefully, they'll have what I want on the lot."

"Oh, I'll arrange the children who need evaluating to come to this building. You won't need to drive around until after Christmas break. How would that be?" Mrs. Verdin seemed eager to accommodate me in any way she could.

"My husband can drop me off here before he goes to work on the Air Force Base. Using a room here to test the children would work well. Having a place here will prevent the distractions they might have in their school."

"Wonderful. Let me show you around and introduce you to a few people in the special education department."

We left her office and walked to a large room with multiple desks. There were several people writing reports. Two were special education teachers who did evaluations, along with one school psychologist and a couple of speech therapists. Then we walked to the other end of the building and entered a smaller office with two desks. Just then a young man came rushing in. "This is our physical therapist, Tim," Bobby said. "You will be sharing this office with him." He and I shook hands. Tim grabbed some papers and headed down the hall.

"You will be our only OT, just as Tim is our only PT. You will cover thirteen district schools, the school on the Air Force Base, as well as the reservation school. I know it's a lot to ask, but there just aren't any therapists available, partly because we have no OT school here in the state."

"OK, I'll do the best I can, but that's a lot for one person. Are there any OT assistants?" I asked.

"Unfortunately, no. We are still advertising, and I remain hopeful, but there have been few responses to our ads." Bobby confided. "OTs are very difficult to find in New Mexico. We know of one other occupational therapist in town, but she only does early intervention and will not work in schools. Her husband is a physical therapist at Holloman, the Air Force Base."

As Bobby mentioned, at that time there was no OT school in New Mexico, and the OT school at the University of Texas at El Paso was in the first stage of development. Alamogordo was also where the New Mexico School for the Blind was located. When I got settled a little and bought a new car, I would meet the director at the School for the Blind. But that was later.

Chapter 21

Jimmy

"There is one youngster I hope you will evaluate when you come in on Monday," Mrs. Verdin said. "The child's mother has been hounding us since the beginning of school to get him into our special education program. She says he has all kinds of problems."

"I'll be glad to do that. How old is he?" I asked.

"He's twelve."

"Do we have testing materials available for that age?"

Mrs. Verdin took me to a closet where tests were kept, and I checked to see what I might use. I decided to perform clinical observations as well as the Bruininks-Oseretsky Test of Motor Development. This test is good for people up to twenty years of age. I would also use a Draw-A-Person test, and ask Jimmy for some writing samples.

When Jimmy arrived with his mother, his mother wanted to brief me all about Jimmy's problems.

"I would prefer to do the evaluation before you share that information with me," I said. "We will be done in about an hour, or an hour and a half, if you wouldn't mind coming back then, I'd appreciate it."

Jimmy's mother left in a bit of a huff. Jimmy and I watched her leave, then began all the large motor tests. I needed him to skip, hop, jump, and walk a straight line on the floor.

In addition, I had set up test materials on a table. I checked for infantile reflexes and found a slight asymmetrical tonic neck reflex, but it did not seem to bother Jimmy when he was writing, drawing, or doing other tabletop activities. His tactile sense seemed okay also. Jimmy seemed very compliant through all the testing.

Later, I talked to Mrs. Verdin about the results, I did not really see any reason from a motor development perspective that required therapy. "I'm afraid we might need to put him on the schedule anyway, maybe for some emotional support. I'm concerned that his mother will sue the school district if we don't provide some therapy for him."

With that, I worked with Jimmy on some fine motor skills, and provided some emotional support. I also helped him learn about friendships. He visited my house to mow the lawn one Saturday and have lunch with us, too. After lunch, I drove him home, and he seemed reluctant to get out of the car. His mother came out and yelled at him, "Get in the house," she screamed, "It is too hot to be outside. You could get heat stroke!"

Much, much later, after I left the school district, we all learned that Jimmy's mother was diagnosed with Munchausen Syndrome, now called Factitious Disorder. She projected her illnesses or disabilities onto Jimmy. She encouraged everyone to think that Jimmy had many different illnesses or disabilities. Jimmy was never ill or disabled, but because it was often implied that he did, he and his mother spent many hours with a variety of doctors,and therapists. Jimmy's mother tried to convince all of us that Jimmy had medical problems. By the time I saw Jimmy, he was angry, but I did not know just how angry he was. Jimmy rarely demonstrated anger during our time together or in the classroom.

Sometimes anger explodes. I later learned that Jimmy had beaten up a kindergartener while they were waiting for the school bus. During the investigation, a psychiatrist became involved in the case. He soon diagnosed Jimmy's mother with Factitious Disorder which caused Jimmy's suppressed anger. It was sad that he suffered for her problems.

Chapter 22

Trevor

Although I was not yet officially trained in Neurodevelopmental Treatment (NDT) techniques, I had worked with several therapists who were. I learned through their clinical guidance. With that background, I was assigned to evaluate Trevor, a seven-year-old boy with cerebral palsy. He was going through kindergarten for the second time. After reading the teacher's information, it was clear that Trevor's primary problem was his absence from the classroom.

Trevor lived with his grandparents. His parents had separated shortly after he was born, and neither of his parents could care for him. Both parents suffered from drug and alcohol overuse. A court order sent Trevor to live with his father's parents when his mother left the family. His father was sent to jail on a misdemeanor charge. His grandparents were both high school graduates, but had no higher education. His grandfather, Adam, had retired after working as an auto mechanic most of his adult life. His grandmother was involved in church activities but had never worked outside the home.

Although Trevor was able to walk, the spasticity in his legs made walking unsteady and incredibly slow. To use the school bathroom, which was far from his classroom, his slow pace took nearly an hour away from the classroom. Because Trevor usually walked to the bathroom at least twice a day, he missed important lessons.

After timing him on a bathroom trip, I decided that an electric wheelchair would greatly improve the efficiency of Trevor's bathroom visits, and thus increase the amount of time he spent in the classroom. From my initial assessment, he had good fine motor development and appeared to be intelligent. I thought Trevor should be in first grade at least. After talking with one of the school psychologists, she told me that Trevor was probably a brighter-than-average youngster, although she had not yet done formal testing. The psychologist used her experience and intuition to informally assess Trevor. As there was no physical therapist available to work with Trevor, I would be the treating therapist.

Physicians in Albuquerque visited schools to provide clinical evaluations for children in the district. I suggested an electric wheelchair for Trevor. A physician prescription was needed for that chair.

"He doesn't need an electric wheelchair," the young orthopedic surgeon said. "What he needs is more therapy."

"Well, I agree that he needs more therapy. However, he's losing too much time away from class just getting to and from the bathroom. It's slowing his school progress. He also can't get out on the playground with the other kids. Trevor needs that socialization."

"I'm not going to write a prescription for a wheelchair, electric or otherwise." The physician seemed determined that a wheelchair would be a hindrance, not a help.

"Let me ask you something: Would you rather have the use of your hands or your legs?" I could see he was taken by surprise. Apparently, he was not used to his decisions being challenged. However, to his credit, the doctor pondered my question.

After thoughtful consideration he said, "I'll write the script for an electric wheelchair." He shrugged and wrote the prescription, which he handed to Trevor's grandfather, Adam, who was at the clinic with Trevor and me.

As Trevor, Adam, and I walked to the next room to see the physical therapist, Adam asked where I expected him to get the money for an expensive electric wheelchair.

"Don't worry about it," I assured him. "There are plenty of places where we can get funding. You may have to come up with a few bucks, but I'm sure we can find nearly full payment from a charitable organization like the Elks Club."

"I don't like to take charity," Adam said.

"Well, it's not charity. It's giving Trevor the opportunity to excel in school. He shouldn't be repeating grades when he doesn't have to. Trevor is plenty bright and shouldn't waste all his class time just getting to and from the bathroom."

"When you put it like that…" Adam and Trevor went in to see the physical therapist.

With the help of a social worker, we found funding and ordered the wheelchair. When the chair arrived, the PT and I helped Trevor learn how to operate his new chair. The teachers were pleased because Trevor was finishing more work. I adjusted my schedule and helped him in class, so he wouldn't miss class time during his OT sessions. He began catching up with the other students. He moved ahead quickly in reading skills. His printing improved as well.

In April, well after Trevor was comfortable with his electric wheelchair, I received a phone call from the principal. There was a problem. I joined a meeting with him and Trevor's grandfather after school dismissed at 2:30.

The principal told us that Trevor was becoming the playground bully. He and a couple of his friends had become a recess terror. Trevor's friends would pick up rocks from the playground and hand them to Trevor, who would throw the rocks at others. He also chased children, trying to run them down with his chair.

"I never thought I'd get a phone call from school saying my grandson was a playground menace," Adam said. He was not pleased.

"I guess I need to teach about playground rules," I said. "I sure didn't realize he would be using his wheelchair to chase other kids, improve his throwing, or try to run them over. I'm sorry."

"Oh, I can discipline him, too," Adam said.

My next fear was that Trevor was in for a spanking or worse. "How about just a good talking-to?" I said to Adam.

"You bet I'll give him that. I just hope I don't laugh in the process," Adam said. "I thought he'd never show us that he's just like me when I was a kid. I always felt sorry for him. I guess I can stop that right now. Trevor won't be throwing any more rocks or trying to run over other kids when I get done with him."

The principal banned Trevor from recess for the rest of the week. This punishment showed that rules applied even to those with a disability. Adam approved. He hoped that Trevor's friends would stay inside at recess as well.

Adam and I left the principal's office together. "You know, Trevor is outside more at home, too," Adam told me. "He even went fishing with me a couple of weekends ago. I've been asking him to do that since he was five, but he never wanted to go. The walk from the car was too difficult. Now Trevor wants to join me because he can use his chair to get near the water. We don't let him use it in the house, but he sure does like going to the park near our house, and he loves coming to school now, too. I'm glad you talked me into getting that thing for him."

"Well, we'll straighten out the playground incidents. After staying inside a couple of times, I'm sure that will end his behavior issue."

Trevor was a fast learner and realized throwing rocks was wrong. He still liked to play tag, but he no longer tried to run anyone over on the playground.

By the end of the school year, Trevor's grades had improved. He was promoted to the first grade, just as he should have been the previous year. If only he'd had the right equipment in the beginning, he never would have repeated kindergarten. I was satisfied that he would be doing well in school from then on. Trevor still needed some therapy, mostly from the PT to improve walking short distances. He probably would not need OT, except for some initial positioning at the beginning of each school year. With that, Trevor would be sure to work at his desk. It seemed a good outcome for Trevor. I was very happy with the cooperation from the physician, principal, physical therapist, and Adam.

Chapter 23

Negotiation

At the end of the school year, I met with the Director of Special Education. I told her that I needed a bigger salary if I was going to continue working for the sprawling school district. Since we had bought a new car and also a house, and Everett no longer had a housing allotment. We needed a better income. Several jobs had opened in Las Cruces, approximately fifty miles from Alamogordo. Mrs. Verdin frowned, then asked me how much I would like.

"I would appreciate at least $30,000 per year," I said.

"We can't pay that much unless you have a master's degree."

"Well, I'd love to have a master's degree, but there are no occupational therapy schools in New Mexico."

"There is a master's degree in Early Childhood Special Education at New Mexico State University in Las Cruces. If you applied and got accepted, maybe I can convince the school board to increase your salary for the coming year."

"That sounds good to me."

"I will even provide references for you from myself and a couple of other staff members here if you're really interested. I know the applications for next semester need to be in next week. I even have their forms in my filing cabinet."

"Oh, gosh! Would you mind giving me one right now? I'll fill it out tonight, write for my transcripts from Grays Harbor

Community College and the University of Puget Sound and get those requests in the mail tomorrow."

The following week, I drove over to New Mexico State University and talked with several faculty members in the Department of Special Education. They had a speech therapy program, but no other therapy programs at the college. One instructor was especially helpful and encouraged me to work on a master's degree in Special Education. An occupational therapist had never applied to their department. Maybe I could contribute to the class with my professional experience.

All master's degree classes were in the evening. Most began at 6 p. m. and lasted until 9 or 10 p.m. With the drive to and from the school across Highway 70 to Las Cruces, I would not arrive home until at least 11 p.m. on class nights. Even so, Everett and I decided that would be all right, and I should begin the master's degree program in the fall of 1990, if I was accepted.

Mrs. Verdin persuaded the school board to increase my salary to $35,000.00 per year. I guess my work impressed them. My results spoke for themselves. The additional money was justified because the school district had hired an occupational therapy assistant from Pennsylvania. I would be busy. I would work with students, supervise the OT assistant, and begin work on the master's degree.

The summer raced by. I worked during the summer school session, and was able to take a trip to Washington State to visit family between the end of summer school and the beginning of the fall session. I spent some time at our family cabin on Puget Sound and relaxed in our front yard enjoying the water, viewing Mt. Rainier across the bay and seeing deer eat apples from the trees in our backyard. I only saw Fritz one evening for dinner, as he was working long hours for the state legislature broadcasting system.

I returned to Alamogordo, ready to begin the new school year and the master's degree program, too. One of the Special Education Department secretaries started her degree in Special Education as well. We planned to drive to Las Cruces together one night a week through the fall semester. The companionship would make the trip easier and fun.

The OT assistant and I reviewed some of the necessary things required for me to supervise her. She needed to work in the same school where I was. We were fortunate the New Mexico State law did not insist that the OT had to be in the same room with the OT assistant. Often, I was writing a report or doing an evaluation of a student while she worked with a child in a classroom.

The class I took at NMSU concentrated on special education laws. It was an easy one for me, as I had studied those extensively when they were passed nationally, in the State of Washington, and then in Alaska, too. New Mexico laws were similar to the other state laws for special education.

Interest in special education was growing across the country. I learned that one of the faculty from the University of Washington in Seattle was hired by the University of New Mexico in Albuquerque to develop an Occupational Therapy Department. Also, two occupational therapy assistant programs were beginning. One of the new programs was set up in Silver City and the other in the eastern part of the state. I was thrilled. In the next four or five years, New Mexico would have their own OT programs. Local people would be hired to fill so many needs in hospitals, school districts, outpatient clinics, and nursing homes.

After the first semester of the school year, I realized that the drive to and from the University was taking its toll. I decided to rent a small apartment in Las Cruces where I could stay the night and drive back to Alamogordo the following day. I would get better rest and time alone for some homework. Everett was

OK with that decision. I would rent for five months. I found a place on the west side of Las Cruces that allowed short-term renters. My little oasis was a single bedroom apartment with a kitchenette and dining counter. It was furnished, too.

When my second semester at NMSU began, the secretary and I would not drive together. Her classes were scheduled on different days, and she needed to be home at night. I was able to arrange my schedule in Alamogordo so that I never had to drive all the way to the Mescalero Apachie Reservation on a day I had night classes. I was putting enough miles on my car each day as it was.

I did not rent the apartment long. On my first night there, I was invaded by roaches. It was so disgusting that I ended up driving home anyway. Once the roach situation was somewhat handled, I stayed for a month, but quickly decided I'd rather drive home after class.

Chapter 24

Neurodevelopmental Treatment Course

The Neurodevelopmental Treatment (NDT) course was to be offered in Albuquerque in the spring of 1991. The director of the children's center in Puyallup, Washington wanted me to take that course years ago. I declined because it was too expensive. In addition, I would not be paid while spending two straight months at the course in Seattle.

In New Mexico, the course was being split with one month in March and one month in June. This was easier to fit into my schedule. I thought I could manage that. I discussed the possibility with Mrs. Verdin. I would take a semester off from the master's degree program. I talked to the Director of Special Education at New Mexico State University as well as my supervisor at the university. I was given permission by all three. Now I would take the month of March off to study the NDT course in Alburquerque.

An occupational therapist I met in Las Cruces was planning to stay at her mother's house in Alburquerque during March and June. She invited me to stay at her mother's home also. Her mother had a lovely four-bedroom home. An additional therapist from Texas stayed there as well. The three of us got to the house on Sunday evening and ate a small dinner. The first week we attended lectures. On Friday night we returned to our own homes.

During the second through fourth week, we arrived in Alburquerque on Sunday night, shared what we had done over the weekend, which in my case was mostly laundry, grocery shopping, and house cleaning. MaryJo from Texas always had more fun. She usually described weekend trip in New Mexico.

During the second through fourth weeks, we heard lectures in the mornings, then in the afternoon, we often worked with children who had cerebral Palsy. (Cerebral Palsy is a neurological disorder. Signals from the brain to muscles are interfered with or inconsistent. A child's movement is either restricted by spasticity or low muscle tone.) The children were brought to the clinic by a parent. The parents were happy with the free therapy. We were helping the children even though we were practicing how to apply what we had learned that morning. We completed the first month of the course, then returned to our regular jobs in April and May.

In June we were back in Alburquerque. We split into groups of four students and one mentor. Each group worked with a child. The mentor guided our work and explained what we were doing well and what needed improvement. Things did not always go well. One six-year-old child had severely tight muscles. We played, laughed, and helped him use a slide. He did not have speech, so he could not tell us to stop doing what we were doing. One thing the instructors had insisted on was making therapy fun. But our play activities only increased his spasticity.

Seeing that, one of the instructors, a speech therapist who and was not our mentor, came over while we worked with this little boy. The instructor observed what was going on in our treatment session and told us to stop. With his non-verbal agreement, she began moving his arm slowly up and down. His spasticity decreased slightly. When the session ended, she assigned us a different child.

The speech therapist worked with that child for the remainder of the course. She took the child into a small room, away from all the other children. When the classes were nearly finished, the intervening speech therapist came to us. She told us to meet her in the small room where she worked with the first youngster.

"You all were doing what you learned from the lectures, but you were not doing what this youngster needed. He needed to work in a quiet place, away from all the activity in the large treatment area. He had to be handled slowly and quietly, or he would be overly stimulated. That is why his muscles tightened more as you all worked with him."

"We were doing what we learned from the lectures," one of the student physical therapists said.

"Yes, I know, but you were not using your own intuition and thinking skills. You must be able to recognize the impact on your patient and adjust to what the patient really needs, not just do what the teacher tells you."

After that, we got a full lecture about using our own observation skills to treat our clients. Applying appropriate observation was valuable even though that might conflict with what an instructor told us.

I had trusted my perceptions often before, but not usually when I was taking a class. I remembered back to the class at the University of Washington which I nearly flunked because I was using my intuition and not following protocol. It can be a tricky balance.

At the end of June we took a written test and a practicum test. I passed the written test without any trouble. In the practicum, we demonstrated our skills using a Raggedy Ann-type doll. I didn't do well, but I passed. I was awarded my certificate with the other students at a small ceremony on the last day of June. I knew that I would use some of the techniques I learned with at least two youngsters in the Alamogordo School District.

Chapter 25

Additional Work

In the fall of 1990, I drove to the Mescalero Reservation twice a month. As usual, my first visit was to conduct evaluations. I walked into the Reservation grade school. In the hall next to the principal's office, six young boys sat on the floor with their heads pressed against the wall. They did not try to look at me. I entered the principal's office and asked the secretary about the boys in the hallway.

"Oh, those boys must have gotten into trouble in their class, and they are being disciplined," she replied. "I'll let the principal know you're here."

In a few minutes, she and the principal came out of his office. He shook my hand. "I'll show you the room you can use for testing."

We walked down the hallway to a room near the back of the school. It was very small, but it had a desk and two chairs. He handed me a couple of folders with information about the two children I was to evaluate that day.

"I can get the testing done today, but I'll have to take the paperwork back to Alamogordo to score the tests and write the report. I can call you to let you know what I found and if therapy is recommended. Then I will treat the child, or children on my next visit, which won't be for another two weeks. When I come back, I can also give the teacher some therapy activities for the classroom. Does that sound OK with you?"

"Yes. We must get permission from the parent, or parents. We will have their signatures before you return in a couple of weeks."

In the following weeks, the school usually scheduled one evaluation and at least three or four children to treat. As promised, I also directed the teachers about occupational therapy activities to be done in the classroom. Sometimes, I just recommended that a student be given a different seating arrangement to provide more stability or fewer distractions.

The Reservation school always found at least four children to punish by sitting in the hall with their heads on the wall. I was upset that there were no other disciplinary methods. I complained to the principal. I suggested that talking to a youngster, especially the older ones, about behavior might work better. Calm talking would not be so demeaning.

"I have been teacher, then principal at this school for twenty years, he said with a scowl. "And most of the teachers here have been with us for ten to fifteen years also. We know what we are doing, and we don't need some outside therapist to tell us how to discipline these kids."

"Oh, I am so sorry." I was startled by his tone. I was going to be the school therapist for only another couple of weeks, so I quit trying to change anything there. For my part, I made sure I gave the children the respect I thought they deserved. Maybe I was cowardly, but I never mentioned how others treated the children again.

After I left the Alamogordo School District and was working in Las Cruces, I read a newspaper article about a young man who burned down the Mescalero Apache Reservation school. With the school gone, the children were sent to either Tularosa schools or to the Ruidoso schools. Local police arrested a graduate of the Reservation school for arson. He was sent to jail for several years.

Many years later, I was in Alaska on a vacation with my husband, Everett. We stayed at an Anchorage hotel, and I began chatting with the coffee shop manager. We talked about places we lived and where we grew up. Coincidentally, the coffee shop manager had grown up on the Mescalero Reservation. I told him about my experience there.

"Oh, you know the school was burned down."

"Yes, I learned of that after I'd moved to Las Cruces."

"Well, the kid who set the fire was a good friend of mine. We were all so angry about the way we were treated. He just had to do something to get back at the teachers and principal. That's why he burned the school down, so other kids would be sent to better schools and be treated better."

"That doesn't surprise me. I was angry myself when I saw those punishments. I hope your friend is doing all right now."

"Yes, he lives in Santa Fe and does quite well now. He's much happier, works full time, and is married, too."

I was happy to learn that the reservation school was never rebuilt, and all the children on the reservation still go to local schools off the reservation.

Chapter 26

Spring 1992

Next on my learning agenda was a weekend workshop on the Miller Assessment for Preschoolers. This time the workshop was in Tularosa, just north of Alamogordo. A couple of the speech therapists, the physical therapist and I decided to attend. We car pooled which made a comfortable change. The presenter was a young man who worked with Dr. Miller's center in Colorado. At the end of the weekend, those of us from Alamogordo felt better prepared for another kindergarten screening. We were also more collaborative evaluating the preschoolers entering the district.

We approached Mrs. Verdin to suggest team evaluations of the younger children. This would model the work I had done in Alaska at the Early Intervention Program. Mrs. Verdin was delighted with a team approach. It not only saved time for us therapists, it allowed parents to bring in a child for only one initial screening. Our teamwork saved busy parents considerable time in appointments and travel, too.

I was back to being the only occupational therapist in the school district. The Certified Occupational Therapy Assistant missed her family and returned to her home in Pennsylvania. This created extra work for me.

Mrs. Verdin was being generous with my time as well. She contracted with the Cloudcroft and Tularosa schools. I was asked to do evaluations in those schools, as well as the Alamogordo schools and the school at Holloman Air Force

Base. With all that, as well as taking classes at NMSU, I barely had time to do my homework.

Because of my experience in the field, I must admit that my classes at NMSU seemed rather easy, not at all what I had expected. One evening my NMSU supervisor asked to speak with me after class. Dr. Gaigoes wondered if I knew of any parent who would be willing to come to the class and share her experiences. She wanted my classmates to hear a parent's perspective of dealing with schools and a handicapped child. I was the only OT who had ever taken classes in her department, and most students in the master's program didn't know the parents of their students. If they were teachers or speech therapists in the school, the only time they met parents was after an evaluation, or during an Individual Education Plan (IEP) meeting. Those short meetings did not allow therapists or teachers to get to know parents very well.

"I may know some parents who might be willing to do that," I told her. One parent who came to mind was particularly articulate. Her now four-year-old son had a bad reaction to his vaccinations as an infant, which left him nearly blind and hypotonic (meaning his muscles were somewhat flaccid). He was unable to speak, and he was prone to seizures. Francis had to advocate for him consistently and finally received medical, as well as financial benefits for him. I told the professor I would ask that mother to speak to the class.

Francis said she loved the idea of speaking to my graduate class. She had experience speaking to the Elks Club in Las Cruces, to early intervention therapists, and to other parents. Francis had never talked with graduate students. I called my professor and told her that Francis would speak to our class. We established a date and I confirmed it with Francis.

"Barring any unseen eventuality," she said with a chuckle. "Do you want me to bring Evan?"

"Probably not. But you can bring pictures, which we could put on a screen, so we could see how he has changed over the years, if you don't mind."

Class was on Wednesday. When I arrived, Francis was already talking with Dr. Gaigoes. It was decided that Dr. Gaigoes would introduce Francis. Time for questions after Francis' initial talk would be allowed. That sounded great to me. I could sit back and twiddle my thumbs, as I'd probably heard most of what Francis would say before at school meetings, and sometimes on the phone after school hours. Francis was never one to keep still if something bothered her about the school's role with Evan. She was quick to pick up the phone in the evening and give me a call.

Graduate students began filling the classroom. Dr. Gaigoes had invited other students in the Special Education Department to listen to Francis' talk. It would be valuable to hear a parent's perspective.

Francis started describing how Evan had been born a normal infant, weighing seven pounds nine ounces, and was eighteen inches long. Labor had been pretty typical—no breach birth, or longer than average labor. She had one older child, a girl.

Evan's first six weeks were normal. He ate well and gained weight. Then he took his first round of vaccinations. Suddenly Evan was fussy, quit eating for a while, and ran a fever for several days after the shots. After the next series of vaccinations at three months, Evan developed seizures. The seizures started hours after his shot. Francis and her husband rushed him to the emergency room when the seizures began, so when he quit breathing, Evan luckily got immediate help. After he stabilized, Evan seemed to be doing better and was sent home.

But troubles continued. Evan's physical development regressed. He lost his eyesight. Although he was put on seizure medication, he would have frequent small seizures daily. At this point, at age four, he needed constant care. His muscle tone was low except when he was having a seizure. He took multiple medications and was fed via a tube connected to his stomach. He wore diapers. He was either in bed,or in his wheelchair. He made sounds, but did not speak.

Francis depicted a long, drawn-out battle to get services for Evan. She also worked to find funding from the resources provided by the makers of the vaccines. She said that many parents did not know funding was available, mostly because it was difficult to prove that the vaccines delayed development. She often talked to parents she met in Albuquerque about this issue, telling them they had to fight long and hard to get these special funds.

After Francis finished talking and disclosing how difficult it was to adjust to a child who was so handicapped, students sat quietly. Then the first question was asked. I don't recall what that question was, I just remember that once a question was asked, many more followed. Finally, Dr. Gaigoes had to say, "Sorry, no more questions. We must all get home sometime tonight and the building will be locked shortly." Class was dismissed.

On the drive home, I thought about the importance of Francis's information. I was amazed at how most of my fellow graduate students had no clue about children's disabilities and the family implications. As a pediatric therapist, I had regular discussions with parents. But teachers rarely had that opportunity, even in the I. E. P. meetings. Being trained to think of all aspects of a person's life, roles, and occupations was a real advantage. That perspective allowed any therapist to work more effectively, not only with the child, but with the family as well.

Chapter 27

Las Cruces

In the Fall of 1992, Everett started engineering classes at New Mexico State University, and I was still working on my degree as well. We decided to move to Las Cruces. I found a job with the Las Cruces School District, and we started looking for a house. Soon after school began for both of us, our Alamogordo house sold, and we found a wonderful house in Las Cruces across town from the University. Even though the house was far across town from the main campus, it was only a block from the street that took us directly to the Engineering School parking lot.

In the beginning, my work at the Las Cruces School District began with only four schools. Other occupational therapists and a couple of OT assistants also worked in the district. My assistant was tall, thin, and elegantly dressed. Her husband was a lawyer. Roberta seemed a bit distant. As we traveled around to various schools, I realized she was not as passionate about her work as I was about mine. We got along OK, but it was not a "chummy" relationship.

A new administration was hired to manage the school district in the fall of 1992. They were particularly focused on the therapy department. Our new administrator wanted to improve both communication among therapists and documentation of service delivery. Some of the records I read were missing critical pieces of information such as test results and adequate plans for classroom intervention. In some cases, paperwork showed little formal testing. I realize that intuition and experience are wonderful things, however I also know that formal testing is a critical part of treatment decision-making.

With that in mind, I decided to see each child on my caseload before assigning them to my OT Assistant. Since Roberta had been working in the district for over a year, I asked her to familiarize me with the various schools and to introduce me to some of the teachers. I thought that would give me a chance to get to know her better. There's nothing like driving around with someone to get acquainted, especially before cell phones were a constant.

After our day together, I knew some children could be assigned to her. I had made a list of children I could assign to her. As we were going over the list, Roberta told me, "I don't like that school. I won't go there."

"Ah, we were given that school, and both of us are assigned to provide services there," I replied. I was shocked that she was asserting herself in this manner by flatly refusing.

"What don't you like?" I asked. "I'd rather not say," Roberta replied as she checked her lipstick.

"Well, if we're going to work together, I think you'd better tell me what other schools you refuse to provide services in," I said flatly.

"No other schools, but there is one teacher in the preschool here that I'd rather not work with."

"OK. Anything else I should know?"

"I can't think of anything, except I need to be home by 3:30,ff so I need to leave now. Bye." She got up and walked out of the room.

I watched her exit with my mouth hanging open.

I stood there for a minute overcome with amazement at her callous and unprofessional attitude. Another therapist came into the room, "How was your day?" she asked.

“Interesting,” I said, and turned back to my desk. I piled more paperwork on it and pretended to be busy. How was I going to work with Roberta? I wasn’t sure if I could even talk with anyone in the department about her. Maybe she’d always been determined to suite her own schedule and her likes and dislikes. Finally, I decided to give her some slack. After all, she had been with the district longer than I had. If she was that bad, wouldn’t they have fired her by now? I packed up a couple of things and headed for dinner before my evening class.

I found a wonderful deli in the mall where I could get a piece of chicken and a salad for a reasonable price. At one of the nice booths, I would spread out my books, and notebooks, and work on some papers while I ate dinner, then head for class at NMSU. I still wasn’t feeling very challenged by this program, but I learned a different perspective on special education and on educational philosophy. That, combined with my working with children in the classroom, broadened my perspective. And the school situations were beginning to change. When I first worked in the school districts years ago, occupational therapists always tookchildren out of the classroom. Now work was shifting to the classroom to support the educator. A fuller classroom experience with other children was valuable to a child with disabilities.

The Director of the Special Education Department called another meeting for 8 a.m. I settled into a seat next to Sally, one of the other OTs. Roberta was absent. The Director said she observed that communication within the department was not what she hoped. To improve, we would all take the Meyers-Briggs Personality Test. With those results, perhaps we could understand each other better and improve our inter-department communication. We would be tested on Wednesday at 4 p.m.

“Darn,” I thought, “there goes my dinner.” I had class at 6 p.m. on Wednesdays. Just as we were being dismissed, Roberta sauntered in. “What’s going on?” she asked.

"Didn't you get the message about a meeting today?" I asked.

"Oh, come to think of it, I think I did."

"Well, what happened?" I said, peeved a bit.

"I guess I forgot," she said and walked away to gather folders of children she was supposed to see that day.

I followed her to the filing cabinet. "We have been instructed to be here next Wednesday to take the Meyers-Briggs. I think you had better make plans to be here then. I'll leave a note on your desk to remind you." I walked away to pick up my things and leave for the day.

All the way to the college, I fumed at Roberta's disinterested and disrespectful attitude. By the time I arrived at campus, I had controlled my feelings and breezed into the school with a smile on my face. It was time to focus on learning something new, listening to an interesting lecture, and trying to apply it to my role as an OT.

All the employees in the Special Education Department took the Meyers-Briggs and the results were in. There was another meeting, but this time it was just with therapists. We had already gone over our individual results with the Director, now it was time to discuss with each other. I had gone through this process at the Children's Therapy Unit in Washington State. It had been somewhat helpful then, and I was hoping it would be helpful now, especially with Roberta. Again, Roberta showed up after the meeting started, but only five minutes late.

While we reviewed personality markers, it turned out that one therapist was my complete opposite. "No wonder, I never understand what you're telling me." I laughed. "So how can we communicate with each other better?" I asked.

"Well, you could ask me when you don't understand," she said.

"Interesting. Except I might think I understand what you're saying, but I really don't. So when that happens, how can I even ask?" I replied.

"Oh, I didn't think of that."

None of my colleagues knew that I had already applied for another job. Before we decided to buy the house in Las Cruces, I interviewed for a job at a nursing home and rehabilitation facility north of Las Cruces.

It was not long before uncomfortable changes were announced within the Special Education Department in Las Cruces, one of which was my resignation.

Roberta came over to me right away, "You're leaving?" She sounded surprised.

"Yes, I have another job."

"But you just got here. I thought you'd be here a long time."

"Well, you were wrong on that count," I said as I gritted my teeth. Roberta left, and I turned to finish clearing out my desk. It was amazing to me that Roberta even acknowledged I was leaving.

"You kind of sound astonished about Roberta," Sally said as I stuffed candy and paperwork—but no student folders—into a box. "Roberta used to gloat about how easy you were to fool. You know that she sometimes went to a sale at Macy's instead of treating one of her assigned kids, didn't you?"

"No. I didn't know that. Well, not my problem now."

"I'll miss you," Sally added.

"It's not like I'm moving away. I'll still be in town and see you at OT meetings," I said. I picked up my cardboard box and left the office. A few weeks later, I heard that Roberta was also no longer with the department. She had been let go when the new director showed up and discovered that Roberta was not in the school building where she was assigned. She was shopping!

Chapter 28

Another Nursing Facility

Less than a year before finishing my Master of Arts in Early Childhood Special Education, I changed jobs yet again. This time I went to work in a nursing home and rehabilitation center in Mesilla Valley, just ten miles north of Las Cruces. It was a lovely, tranquil setting where the agricultural products mostly consisted of cattle, corn, and chilis. Irrigation ditches moved water from the lower flow of the Rio Grande into the fields near the facility. Most of the farms were worked by long-standing immigrants from Mexico.

The physical therapist, Rita, and the speech therapist, Kate, had been working there for several months before I arrived. Kate and I hit it off quickly. Fortunately, she was bilingual, as I still only knew a few words of Spanish. When I needed a translator during evaluations, she was always willing to assist me. Kate taught me to understand the difference between those who prided themselves in being original descendants of the 1600's Spanish settlers in this country and those who had recently immigrated from Mexico. With Rita and Kate's support, I got oriented quickly. There were few changes in the delivery of occupational therapy services between the time I left Our Lady of Compassion Care Center in Anchorage in 1989, and when I started at the nursing home and rehabilitation facility in New Mexico in 1992. The really big changes were yet to come.

My duties included the additional responsibility of serving as a clinical instructor to an occupational therapy assistant student.

Interest and use of occupational therapy continued to grow through legislation that required our services. The University of Texas at El Paso had started an occupational therapy program under the guidance of the University of Texas at Galveston. The UT/El Paso program director came to the nursing home to see the facility and determine if we could help provide field trips and practical experience for students.

The patient load at the nursing home and rehabilitation center was relatively light compared to my work in the schools. I only had one place to go for the day as well, which was a real treat. The drive out to the facility was quiet and peaceful. I enjoyed working with elderly patients again.

Chapter 29

Mrs. McKinley

One of our patients was the former owner of a general store that she had inherited from her parents and later passed on to her son. Mrs. McKinley had suffered a stroke and came to us for rehabilitation. Her children often visited and made a point to consult with her about the business. Kate and I soon realized that Mrs. McKinley was not only the former owner of the store, but was currently the Chairman of the Board of her family's corporation.

At eighty-six years old and somewhat debilitated from her recent stroke, she remained positive, cheerful and very determined to work hard at her recovery. At first, she was somewhat reluctant to perform some of the exercises I had planned. I tried again by designing the exercises as a game. Mrs. McKinley quickly perked up and became eager to see if she could "win." She especially loved trying to knock stacking cones off her tray table while her arm was secured to a movable "skateboard." She knocked the cones off so far, I had to chase after them. The farther she made me go to retrieve the cones the better she liked it. That's how she "won" the game. The exercise helped strengthen controlled movement in her right arm. As a true game-player, she would leave the harder cone hits for the end of the therapy session.

Within a few months, Mrs. McKinley decided she wanted to attend a talk given by the daughter of one of the pioneer ministers to the Mesilla Valley. I thought she would be able to do that. When we discovered that none of her family would be available to take her, I offered to drive her to the event myself. When I arrived that Saturday afternoon, she was not dressed yet. I was furious. I found her nursing assistant and told her that she needed to help me get Mrs. McKinley dressed and ready to go.

"Nobody told me she had an appointment. We usually don't get her dressed until dinner time on Saturdays."

"You what?" I replied.

"I said we don't usually get her dressed until dinnertime'," the nursing assistant repeated.

We finished getting Mrs. McKinley ready to leave the facility when her daughter showed up.

"Turns out I had a change of plans, and I can take Mom to the author event."

"OK, I'll meet you there." I said as we wheeled Mrs. McKinley to her daughter's waiting car. I helped transfer her into the car and watched as they drove away.

We met at St. James Episcopal Church parking lot on the south side of Las Cruces. The author event was lovely. The speaker had written a biography of her father and his itinerant ministry in the Mesilla Valley. He also knit and would often knit as he rode his horse or walked between various churches. His knitting accomplishments included hats, sweaters and shawls as well as blankets which he gave to parishioners who needed them, or to homeless people passing through the community. Mrs. McKinley knew the daughter and her father, Preacher Lewis, when she was growing up because they often shopped at the store her parents owned. They had a pleasant, although brief, visit,, and Mrs. McKinley's daughter bought a couple of copies of the book *Journey of Faith* to share.

She then asked if I could take her mother back to the nursing home as she had several things she needed to do. I said I would.

After getting Mrs. McKinley back into more comfortable clothes, I searched for the nursing assistant. It turned out that she had left for the day, but I made a mental note to apologize for my harshness to her. I made another mental note to find out why she hadn't been informed that Mrs. McKinley had outside plans. And I was puzzled as well about why residents were not usually dressed until just before Saturday dinnertime.

I had other reasons to question the patient services at the nursing home. One afternoon before lunch, the light above the door to Mrs. McKinley's room was on. There was no nursing assistant in sight, so I entered her room. She was in the bathroom sitting on the toilet. "Where is the assistant?" I asked.

"Oh, she went to get some toilet paper. There was none in here, or in my closet."

"Well, I didn't see her in the hallway, so I'll go get some and be right back." I started down the hall and saw the nursing assistant in another resident's room.

"Did you get Mrs. McKinley toilet paper?"

"No," she answered. "I got caught by this gentleman."

"OK. I'll get the toilet paper and get Mrs. McKinley to the dining room in a bit." I hurried to the store room, found three rolls of toilet paper then rushed back to Mrs. McKinley's room.

As I was putting a roll of toilet paper on the holder, Mrs. McKinley said, "No, not that way! I'm a front roller, not a back roller." I realized I was putting the toilet paper onto the holder so that it rolled off toward the wall. I quickly changed it, so the toilet paper came off the front side of the roll.

Later, I had several discussions with people about how they prefer to place toilet paper on the holder. Some are "front rollers", while others are "back rollers". It seems that people do have distinct preferences as to how toilet paper is placed on the holder. That was a lesson well learned.

Chapter 30

Anita

Alzheimer's disease was rarely diagnosed during the early 1990s. Most dementias were attributed to alcohol, some form of brain trauma, or an unknown etiology. When one resident was admitted who had a broken ankle, we were told that she was only at our facility for physical therapy and rehabilitation. However, it soon became clear that there was much more going on with Anita than just a broken ankle. The most notable thing was that we had difficulty communicating with her in either English or Spanish. When her husband came to visit late one afternoon soon after she was admitted, I approached him to see how he was coping and asked him how we might better serve his wife. "Oh, I guess you need to know that she's from Germany. That's where she grew up."

"Given her age, was she anywhere near the troops during World War II?" I asked. When I was a child during WWII, we lived in Seattle, so I experienced the tension of living with impending threats. My own experience of the war was blackout curtains, so important to my dad, who was a civil patrol block warden and a plane spotter. My mother hosted groups of women who rolled bandages for the Red Cross. We also had food and gas rationing, but I couldn't imagine living in an actual European combat zone.

"Anita lived in Berlin. Her father was killed in the war and, she and her mother barely survived on the streets," he said.

"So, she's actually speaking German now rather than English," I said.

"Well, yes, most of the time. Sometimes she will use an English phrase, but she won't understand English when I answer her in English."

"Do you know anyone who might help us communicate with her? Is someone willing to come out here and translate?" I asked.

"Not really. I'm just hoping you guys can get her walking again, as I promised her I'd take her back to Germany just before she broke her ankle. I mean to make good on that promise," he replied.

"OK, we'll see what we can do to help you achieve that goal. I assume you want to take Anita home as soon as she can walk again, is that right?" I asked.

"Yes, I would love to be able to do that," he said. Just then, Anita was wheeled into the physical therapy gym, so I left.

"Kate, do you know anybody who speaks German?" I asked the speech therapist when I saw her in the hall.

"No. I sure don't. Oh wait. I believe the receptionist took German in high school."

Kate and I approached the administrator to see if we might get the receptionist to help out with translating. We could also use someone to talk to Anita as she could sometimes get quite agitated. Hearing someone speak her own language might help calm her down, especially at mealtimes.

The administrator supported us. He found someone else to cover the phones and reception area when we asked the regular receptionist to talk to Anita. Kate and I usually worked with Anita in the dining room as we discovered that another problem was feeding herself. Kate found that Anita had a problem with swallowing when she did her evaluation. When I did my evaluation, I found that Anita had difficulty staying on task. She often spent her mealtime looking around and forgot to eat.

The use of German was very beneficial to Anita and to us. In the few weeks we worked with her, however, her dementia rapidly progressed. Her husband realized he would not be able to take her home, or take her back to Germany. As we had no long-term bed available at our facility, she was discharged to a nursing home in Las Cruces that was closer to their home. Unhappily, within a matter of months Anita became completely bedridden and died at the other nursing home.

I felt sad and somewhat of a failure that we were not able to help her as much as I hoped. At the time there was not a lot of research about the stages and progression of Alzheimer's disease. There was a lot more to learn about that and the coming numbers of people who would be diagnosed with this devastating disorder.

Chapter 31

Dr. Sam

Dr. Sam came into the nursing home twice a week to visit his wife, who had been in the home for several months. Joyce, Dr. Sam's wife, had endured a stroke. She did not respond well to therapy and was no longer being treated. Because of her physical maladies, Dr. Sam could no longer take care of her at home. We communicated about Joyce and her condition, so I knew Dr. Sam a bit, even though his wife was not my patient. Kate and I also thought that Dr. Sam's wife had dementia in addition to her stroke problems.

One day I was given an order to evaluate Dr. Sam. He had fallen and broken his left hip. He was there for physical therapy and occupational therapy after the hip surgery. When I went to evaluate Dr. Sam, he told me he did not need occupational therapy. He knew what OTs did, and he did not have a stroke, or dementia like his wife. He refused to participate in the evaluation. "I can do other things to help you," I said.

"No, you can't. I just need physical therapy to get stronger after my hip surgery. You can go now."

I left his room and called Dr. Sam's physician. I explained that Dr. Sam refused the occupational therapy evaluation. "Well, I guess we'll just have to let him decide what he wants," his physician told me.

Soon after that call, I saw Dr. Sam in the dining room. He had no trouble feeding himself, swallowing, or chewing. He was sociable with other residents and seemed to be doing well. I talked to the physical therapist. She said Dr. Sam was compliant with all the exercises that he was instructed to do. "One thing I am a bit concerned about, however, is that he always wears slippers when he comes to PT. He never wears stockings or shoes. Since he is still mostly using a wheelchair to get around, that isn't a problem, but when he starts walking, I don't know if he will have the flexibility to dress himself, especially get his shoes and socks on."

Time passed. After about a month, I saw Dr. Sam walking down the hall in his slippers. He was shuffling along. His slippers were a bit loose on his feet. He did not have any socks on.

"Hi, Dr. Sam. How come you're not wearing stockings with your slippers?" I asked.

"Oh, I can't put on my socks; I can't reach down to do that."

"How about I show you some things that might help you get your socks on?"

"Can you do that?" he asked.

"I'll get some equipment and meet you in the physical therapy department." In the cupboard of the OT treatment area, I got a dressing stick, a stocking aide, a long-handled shoehorn, and a Reacher. (A Reacher is a three- or four-foot long stick with a tong at one end that closes over an item on a shelf or on the floor. When you pull a hook on the handle, the Reacher closes over the item, and you can pick it up from the floor,or from a shelf.) I took all these items with me to the physical therapy treatment area. Dr. Sam was waiting for me.

"What's all that stuff?" Dr. Sam asked.

"I'll show you. Please take off your slippers."

Dr. Sam used one foot to push the slipper from the other foot. With his feet bare, I held the stocking aide, which is a plastic “U” shaped item with cords attached on each side at the top. I picked up a stocking and showed him how to put the stocking over the plastic “U” shape, then use the cords to let the plastic drop to the floor. He could put his foot into the curve of the “U” and pull on the cords. As he pulled the cords, the stocking fit over his foot. He had a stocking on his foot. With the dressing stick, he picked the end of the stocking and pulled the stocking up his leg. He put the other stocking on his other foot. He concentrated and did not say anything.

“So, what’s that thing for?” he asked, pointing to the Reacher.

“This is for picking up things off the floor if you drop something. Or you can use it to reach something off a shelf that might be too high.”

“OK, let me try that.”

“Let’s finish getting your shoes on first. You don’t want to be walking around in your stockings. You could slip and fall if you do that.”

“True,” he said.

I showed him how to put the long-handled shoehorn into the back of his shoe. Then he could slip his foot into the shoe without difficulty. As he wore shoes that did not need to be tied, that worked well. He got both shoes on.

“Well, I’ll be darned,” Dr. Sam said. “Now I can even walk outside without worrying about slipping in my slippers.”

“Good. You can keep these helpful gadgets to use and even take them home with you when you leave.”

“OK. Now show me how to use that other thing.”

I took the Reacher and purposefully dropped a couple of things on the floor. I showed Dr. Sam how to pick up objects using the Reacher. After dropping a couple of more things on the floor, Dr. Sam got into the spirit. He stood up. With the

Reacher, he picked up the sock, a pillow, and a shirt off the floor.

"That works great! Thanks."

Not long after our little therapy session, Dr. Sam was discharged from the nursing facility. With simple OT tools, he could handle everything at home.

Several months later I was at a grocery store in Las Cruces when I heard, "OT, OT."

I turned around and saw Dr. Sam smiling at me. I asked how he was doing. I hadn't seen him since he was discharged. "I'm doing great! I wanted to tell you that I use those easy aides every day. I couldn't get dressed without them. And that Reacher thing is wonderful. I never worry about falling."

"I'm so glad to hear that."

"I'm just happy that you taught me that there's more to occupational therapy than I ever imagined. Thanks."

We shook hands and I went on with my shopping, glad that I had taught an older doctor something new and useful.

Chapter 32

The Okey Dokey Man

Mr. Connor was admitted to the nursing home and rehabilitation center in Southern New Mexico with a poor prognosis. The doctors did not give him long to live. Despite that, Mr. Connor was placed in the Rehabilitation Unit. To comply with Medicare requirements, evaluations by the physical therapist, occupational therapist and speech therapist, were required. Mr. Connor's severe left cerebral hemisphere stroke caused him to have aphasia, or difficulty speaking. He showed little movement in his right arm and leg. He was on a diet of pureed food, which the nursing assistants fed him.

According to his daughter, Linda, Mr. Connor had been fully independent before the stroke in early December. He had done his own cooking, grocery shopping, and driving. His second wife died of cancer six months before his stroke. Linda's mother died seven years before that. Mr. Connor had cared for both of his wives at the end of their lives.

Linda told us that even with all that, her dad was generally a very positive person. She was reluctant to situate him in hospice (end of life, palliative) care. "I just don't want to think he only has six months to live," she said during the intake meeting. At that meeting, each of us therapists, two nurses, the administrator of the facility, and the doctor did not want to argue with her or even suggest that perhaps Mr. Connor would be better off in hospice care. Linda was the only family member present. There were two other adult children, however, Linda had the legal authority to make life care decisions for her father.

She was also the only family member who lived close enough to attend the meeting.

Kate, the speech therapist, Rita, the PT, and I decided to evaluate Mr. Connor as a team, not only in the interests of time, but also because we would be disturbing him for an hour to an hour and a half rather than three hours straight. We planned our time carefully for the following morning after breakfast.

When the three of us entered Mr. Connor's room at nine, he appeared to be asleep. He lay on his back with the head of the hospital bed only slightly raised. Although we said, "Good morning, Mr. Connor," there was no response.

A tray of food, all liquids, rested on the bed stand next to the bed. Obviously, he had not eaten or been fed, yet according to his chart, he had eaten breakfast. Kate left the room and found the nursing assistant who was supposed to have fed him. When Kate returned, she told us that the nursing assistant had not found time to finish feeding Mr. Connor. The tray had most likely been in his room for over two hours. Two hours for food to sit out was the limit by Medicare standards. Kate took the tray to the kitchen and returned shortly with a fresh tray of food.

While Kate was gone, Rita and I began our part of the evaluation. Rita and I began moving his right arm, and suddenly Mr. Connor opened his eyes, turned his head, and smiled at us. He made good eye contact with Rita, who was nearest to him. She was checking his right shoulder range of motion. I was holding his hand and stabilizing his elbow so it would not flop as Rita moved his upper arm above his head. Rita explained who we were and what we were doing. Mr. Connor grunted, but did not stop smiling. I checked for any grip strength. There was none on the right, and no independent detectable movement in his fingers. The grip strength on his left hand measured ten pounds. His range of motion on the left arm, wrist, and hand was good in all joints. Certainly, that was enough for him to feed himself if Kate determined that his swallowing was safe. She wanted to get some food into him before Rita and I transferred him to the wheelchair. Kate explained what she wanted him to do as she rolled the bedside tray across the bed. We raised the head of the bed into a more upright position, which he seemed to tolerate well. In other words, he did not slump over to the right and did not fall forward. His trunk stability appeared good.

Kate picked up a bowl of warm oatmeal. "Would you like sugar and milk on your cereal?" she asked.

Mr. Connor nodded his head "yes." He placed his left hand on the tray near the spoon.

"Would you like me to feed you?" Kate asked. Mr. Connor smiled but reached for the spoon, so Kate moved the bowl more to his left, and Mr. Connor began feeding himself. He ate eagerly and appeared to have no trouble swallowing. Kate put a straw into a glass of cranberry juice, and held the glass toward Mr. Connor's mouth while stabilizing the straw between her index and middle fingers. Mr. Connor took a drink. Immediately, he coughed. I put my arm behind his shoulders to move him forward while Rita pulled the tray table out of the way, and Kate tipped Mr. Connor's head down. He was able to clear his throat of the juice and get a good breath.

"Looks like you need thickened liquids, and we need to work on swallowing," Kate said. She added some thickening agent to the juice. Mr. Connor took another drink and then swallowed without difficulty. He beamed.

I checked to see that his slippers had non-skid soles before I put them on his feet. Rita and I helped Mr. Connor sit on the side of the bed with his feet on the floor. After nearly a minute, we got him standing, then turned him to sit in the wheelchair. Rita wheeled him down to the therapy gym. Kate and I followed. We discussed better eating utensils for Mr. Connor. We decided that we would work with him together during breakfast and lunch. Kate would help him swallow liquids, and I would encourage Mr. Connor to use some adaptive dining utensils, such as a scoop bowl and perhaps a swivel spoon, or an adapted fork.

Kate went back to our office while I continued to the gym. Rita told me she would work with Mr. Connor on some strengthening exercises for his left leg and arm. Before she did that, he needed a sling to keep his right arm from flopping around. "How about getting dressed, too?" I asked Mr. Connor.

He grinned. Then he said, "Okey Dokey." Both Rita and I laughed in amazement. Those were the first actual words Mr. Connor said. He was almost laughing.

Over the next several weeks, the three of us worked with Mr. Connor. When we asked if he wanted to get up or go to breakfast or lunch, his response was "Okey Dokey." When I asked if he wanted to get dressed, his response was, "Okey Dokey." He smiled often and sometimes frowned when he was not ready to do something, especially with a nursing assistant, or when he did not want to eat something that was served at meals.

His daughter Linda was amazed that he was up and dressed when she arrived. He could select his own clothes, when asked. When handed a shirt, he could put it on himself, dressing his right side first. With minimal assistance, he could put on his khaki pants. He still needed maximum assistance to get into his slippers and to get on and off the toilet from his wheelchair. He now wore absorbent underwear and seemed glad to be finished with the catheter.

Linda was even more surprised that Mr. Connor began to propel himself in his wheelchair to and from his room to activities and meals. His wheelchair was special; it could be propelled from the left side. He used his left foot to draw the wheelchair forward and his left hand to push and to steer. (These days, he probably would have an electric wheelchair with controls on the left side.)

Mr. Connor often attended facility activities, including the popular music performances and Bible study. He worked jigsaw puzzles and played cards using a card holder I had gotten for him. When asked how he was doing, his response nearly always was a broad smile and an "Okey Dokey."

We discharged Mr. Connor from the skilled therapy unit after about two months. Kate, Rita, and I felt he had maximized his therapy progress. He moved to long-term care within the same facility shortly after that. I took a different job, but before I left, I said goodbye to Mr. Connor. He seemed to understand I was leaving, but still all he could do was smile and say, "Okey Dokey." I was glad Mr. Connor seemed to be having a good quality of life in the nursing home and had not been sent to hospice care.

Chapter 33

Water color and a Patient

One afternoon, I exited the back door to walk across the parking lot over to the nursing facility front office. It was a beautiful fall day, and I wanted to be outside a bit. Near the front of the building there was a patient on oxygen, sitting in her wheelchair smoking a cigarette.

"You shouldn't be smoking with the oxygen going into your nose," I said. "That is dangerous."

"Oh, I know, but I really wanted a cigarette, and it's such a beautiful day. They won't let me smoke inside," she said.

I walked into the administrator's office and dropped off some paperwork, then told him about the patient outside. "I'll tell the nurse to go get her," he told me.

Before long the nurse on Mrs. Butler's floor came to ask if I would do something with Mrs. Butler.

"Do you have an order for me to see her?" I asked.

"No, but I'll get one. She needs something to do, and she doesn't seem interested in anything we offer. She doesn't play cards and doesn't really socialize with other patients."

I got the order to treat Mrs. Butler, and found that she could do most things herself. She did, however, say she would like to learn to watercolor. I had done some watercolor painting, but was just an amateur.

"I will get some paints, brushes and the right watercolor paper. We'll set you up in the therapy room. What subject would you like to paint? Maybe I can get that for you too."

"Oh, I'd like to paint flowers," she said.

I already had everything we needed at home. I took a watercolor painting class in Alamogordo before we moved to Las Cruces. I was not trained as an art therapist, but I thought I knew enough to get Mrs. Butler started.

The following day after lunch, Mrs. Butler arrived at the therapy room. I put out the watercolor painting things and a pot of lilies I picked from our flower bed that morning. "Here you go," I said, smiling at her.

"You might want to make a light pencil sketch before you actually paint on this paper."

"OK, I know how to do that. Actually, I used to paint in acrylics and sometimes oil, but I never painted in watercolor."

"I took a watercolor class. My teacher said you need to start with the lightest colors first, then sometimes let the paint dry before adding the darker colors. If you want to mix colors, you should do that in a little tray, here. Or you can actually mix colors on the paper, too."

"Let me have a couple of scrap papers and I can practice."

I put a couple of pieces of watercolor paper on the table in front of her and also got a tray with water for cleaning brushes.

Mrs. Butler seemed to be totally occupied for the next two hours. I treated a couple of patients in the therapy room while she was there. Then I had to treat a patient in her room, so I asked Mrs. Butler to please put the things away and go back to her room, or to the recreation room. I did not want to leave her alone.

The next day, Mrs. Butler returned to the therapy room right after breakfast. I was surprised to see her. My patient seemed interested in Mrs. Butler's painting, so we watched her for a few minutes. My patient said she would like to try that, too. Pretty soon three women painted in the therapy room. Mrs. Butler was the real artist. She found it engrossing.

In fact, Mrs. Butler was no longer going outside to smoke. She hadn't had a cigarette since she started painting. I was glad to hear that.

Six weeks into the painting sessions, Mrs. Butler finished three watercolor paintings, but she no longer came into the therapy room. I went to find out what had happened.

"She is in bed," the nurse told me. "She is not doing very well. Her breathing is worse, and we may have to intubate her."

"Oh, it isn't because of the painting, I hope," I said.

"No. I'm sure not."

Three days later, Mrs. Butler passed away. When I talked to her daughter later, her daughter told me that Mrs. Butler was so happy painting. Her last six weeks had been a real blessing. Then her daughter showed me several sketches Mrs. Butler did even while in bed. "I'm so glad to have these and the paintings she did as well. It's a wonderful remembrance of a productive and happy time."

I never "taught" watercolor painting again.

Now many art therapists work at nursing facilities, rehabilitation centers and children's therapy units. Occupational therapists do not often teach patients painting, drawing or sculpture any longer.

Chapter 34

Jerry

In the fall of 1994, I worked part-time at a pediatric outpatient clinic in El Paso, Texas. The facility was owned by Clarise, a speech pathologist. She told me we had a referral for an eight-year-old with autism who lived in a group home. Jerry was doing well in that environment until about six weeks ago, when suddenly he displayed behavioral issues. He would have bursts of tantrum-like episodes, throw his food at dinner time, punch furniture, and kick aides at dinner and bedtime.

When one of the aides asked him to stop, he ran from the facility and into the street. That was dangerous. It was against their policy to lock the door, and there was no fence. Before I saw him, Jerry was given a general medical exam. The doctor found no physical symptoms such as an ear infection, which could have explained the behavior shift. The doctor and the group home director decided that an occupational therapy evaluation was in order.

I wanted to focus on Jerry's sensory systems. So I prepared a treatment room by turning off the buzzing overhead fluorescent lights and switching on a small lamp. I hung a platform swing from the ceiling hook and set up a table with playdough and a can of shaving cream. I put several food items with different flavors and textures in a cupboard. I met Jerry and two aides in the lobby. I asked what they had observed regarding Jerry's behavior and if there had been any recent changes. "None," according to the male aide. He answered all my questions because he had worked at the group home the longest and knew Jerry well. The female aide busied herself with filling out paperwork.

Jerry made little eye contact, which is typical of those on the autism spectrum. He stood close to the male aide but did not touch him. Although Jerry seemed to be listening, he did not speak – again, not unusual. I addressed Jerry directly. "My name is Margret. Will you come with me?" I waited to see if I would get an answer before I moved. It took nearly a minute. Jerry finally said, "Yes."

We entered the treatment room, just the two of us. Jerry looked around and pointed to the platform swing. He got on it and began swinging around. I asked him to get onto his hands and knees, which he did, and he smiled at me. As I presented different sensory stimuli, he appeared to be having fun. I turned on the overhead lights. They snapped and buzzed. Jerry looked up and put his hands to his ears but did not become agitated. He accepted my deep pressure touch but brushed my hand away and frowned when I touched him lightly on the forearm. I quickly removed my hand. Jerry enjoyed making animals with the playdough but did not want to touch the shaving cream when I squirted some on the table.

I turned on some music. The music I selected had a high pitch. Jerry turned away. Again, he put his hands to his ears but did not become agitated. I could find nothing that disturbed him except light touch and possibly higher pitched sounds. After going through all the sensory systems – motion, touch, both deep pressure and light touch, taste, smell, vision, and hearing – the only disturbances he responded to negatively seemed to be light touch and perhaps higher frequency sound. Jerry did well and did not demonstrate any behavioral problems during the session. He did not kick, flap his hands, or run away.

We finished and joined the aides in the waiting room. The female aide told Jerry to sit down and wait. Immediately, Jerry began flapping his hands, then ran back toward the treatment room. "Let him go," I said. "He'll be fine. Could you answer a couple of questions for me?" I asked the woman.

"Sure," she responded. "What do you want to know?". Her voice was very high pitched and squeaky – like fingernails on a blackboard.

"How long have you worked at the group home?" I asked.

"Nearly two months," she replied.

"What shift do you work?"

"I usually work the late afternoon to midnight shift. I'm in school during the morning."

"OK, let's go find Jerry. I'm sure he returned to the treatment room."

The aides and I walked back to the treatment room. Jerry was spinning on the platform swing. When we entered the room, he looked at me. "It's OK," I said.

He got off the swing and moved as far away as he could from the aides. "That's all I need to know," I said. "We should walk to the exit, but I want the two of you to go first."

The aides left the room. Jerry and I followed. When we arrived at the front door, the director of the group home was there with Clarise, the owner of the outpatient facility. Joe, the director, of Jerry's group home, asked what I found out, if anything. "I think Jerry's problems are sound frequency and light touch. Particularly, a certain voice is setting him off."

"Are you serious?" the Director said.

"Yes. Do you want a demonstration?"

"I do."

I asked the female aide to say something to Jerry. When she did, Jerry began to get agitated. He flapped his hands, then covered his ears.

Speaking to the female aide, I said, "If you could lower your voice, or whisper, I think you would find Jerry would react differently. It appears the pitch of your voice disturbs him."

"I never would have imagined something like that could be the problem. Thank you," Joe said. When they all left the clinic, I noticed that Jerry was in Joe's car as they drove out of the parking lot, and the two aides drove away in another car.

I followed up two weeks later. Joe told me that he had assigned the female aide a different position, so she no longer interacted with Jerry. "Jerry has had no outbursts since we made that change. We never would have figured out the voice problem. We have also been careful to use deep pressure touch when we need to physically help him."

In the past several years, I learned that movie theaters arrange special performances where the sound and lights are adjusted so people with autism can enjoy the show. These adjustments allow those with extreme sensitivity to visual and auditory stimuli the same fun as their peers. We do not usually think of going to movies as an occupation, but it is. We want everyone to live life to their fullest. As an OT, it is encouraging to know that movie theater managers recognize that environmental factors can make a difference for some audiences.

Chapter 35

Richard

In November 1997, Everett and I moved to Massachusetts. Everett finished his degree in electrical engineering and began working in the defense industry.

I moved on to new opportunities and immersed myself in different roles, but my passion for occupational therapy never waned. It was always about bridging the gap between challenges and possibilities, empowering individuals to regain their independence and thrive in their environments. Each patient I worked with left an imprint, teaching me resilience and the value of incremental progress. In Massachusetts, my career took a significant turn, leading me to a new chapter where I faced even more complex cases.

Before we moved, I finished my master of arts at New Mexico State University and taught for a year in the Occupational Therapy Department at the University of Texas at El Paso. I wanted to teach in another OT program. In Massachusetts, most colleges wanted faculty with doctorates. So, I went to work at the Harvard outpatient clinic not too far from our house. The clinic was run by HealthSouth-Braintree Hospital.

I was to evaluate and treat children and adult patients. Again, I was the only OT who was trained in the Southern California Sensory Integration Tests, and I was one of two OTs who worked in the clinic. We attended weekly therapy meetings in Braintree, fifty miles away. We joined four OTs who worked in the Health South Hospital there. They worked mostly with clients who had spinal cord injuries, strokes, or other neurological problems.

In March 1998, we received a referral for a twenty-four-year-old man. Richard was discharged from Spaulding Hospital to his parents' home near the Harvard clinic. He had been in a car accident resulting in a spinal cord injury at the cervical spine joints five and six. His car crashed into a tree.

Richard arrived at the clinic accompanied by his mother, Judith. He was in an electric wheelchair, which he propelled himself by a sip and puff method. (There was a connection near his mouth and the motor on the chair. When he puffed into the tube the chair would move forward. When he sipped into the tube the chair would slow down or stop.) He did not smile or acknowledge me. Judith shook my hand and introduced herself. "I'll fill out the paperwork while you evaluate Richard," she said.

"OK. Richard, let's go down the hall and into one of the treatment rooms," I said.

I had not worked with many spinal cord injured patients, but I was the only OT who had an opening in her schedule. I could consult another OT on staff if I needed to. The therapists down at HealthSouth-Braintree Hospital were also available if I needed more consultation. Richard had been treated as an inpatient at Spaulding Hospital immediately after the crash. That hospital was renowned for successful outcomes for patients with spinal cord injuries and brain trauma.

When Richard and I settled into the treatment room, I asked him what he wanted from therapy.

"I want to feed myself. I'm not a baby, and I can chew and swallow well enough. Right now, Mom or my attendant has to feed me anything solid, and I hate that."

"Well, OK. Is there anything else?"

"Of course. I'd like to walk again, drive a car, and get back to college in September."

"Wouldn't that be nice. I'm not a PT, but getting back to college in September is something we can work on, too. Let's focus on the eating for now, though, OK?"

Richard seemed to relax a bit and smiled at me. "OK."

I checked the amount of movement in his right hand and arm. I checked his shoulder movements. He had fair control of his head movements. His vision was intact, as was his hearing. He did not have any trouble talking and could swallow without difficulty. I did not understand why the OTs at the hospital had not helped him feed himself.

"At least you were able to get the electric wheelchair before you left. You drive that quite well. Did you have speech therapy for any swallowing problems?"

"Yes, but not much. I didn't need much."

I pulled some catalogs of adaptive eating equipment out of the cabinet and laid them on the table.

"Here are pictures of utensils we might use to help you eat. We'll have to order some of them," I said. "A swivel spoon and a scoop bowl are a pretty good combination. The swivel spoon stays horizontal in case your arm jerks unexpectedly."

"I had no idea there was so much stuff," Richard said. "What's that?" He pointed to a sling arrangement that fits onto the back of a wheelchair.

"Oh, that's an arm sling. It allows you to move your arm around using your shoulder and elbow movements. That way you can scoop food from the bowl, then tip your hand up to your mouth."

"Wow. There's some neat stuff in here." I flipped through more pages.

Richard's mother joined us. We showed her some of the items Richard and I thought he could use. "Go ahead and order that equipment," she said. "I need to get to work, and your hour is nearly up anyway. Why don't we wait for the equipment to get here before we see you again?"

We left the treatment room, and I walked out to the van, where Richard rolled into the back. His mother tightened the straps to secure the wheelchair. She had learned all the right moves from the staff at the hospital before Richard was discharged.

As soon as the eating equipment came, we scheduled Richard's second appointment. I requested that they bring in a tray that fit his wheelchair also. Although applesauce was not Richard's favorite food, we began with that. It was obvious that we needed a different tray because Richard nearly pushed the scoop dish off his tray on the first scoop. He needed a bit more control of his arm, and I needed to adjust the over-the-shoulder sling.

I saw Richard for several visits, and made numerous adjustments to the sling apparatus. Richard's father created a tray with a rim to prevent the bowl from sliding off, and soon Richard was eating independently. This was all before the electronic devices that many patients with spinal cord injuries have available now.

I discharged Richard a couple of months later. He had progressed enough to participate in his sister's wedding in June. Judith, his mother, sent me a picture of Richard dressed in his tuxedo and a note that said he was considering returning to college with an aide. Richard was doing very well. I was delighted.

Another month went by, and Judith called to tell me Richard had died. I asked if he had pneumonia and worried that he had aspirated some food.

"No." Judith said. "His catheter developed a twist in it, and he was not able to expel urine. We drove him back to the hospital, but he had an infection. The doctors tried to unkink the catheter and pull it out. They had to operate, and Richard died on the operating table."

"I'm so sorry. I know he was looking forward to going back to school."

"Thank you," Judith said. "Richard was glad that he was able to feed himself finally. You were a great help. It was a team effort, too."

I felt badly that I couldn't have done more, yet during his last months, Richard seemed to accept his limitations and was willing to move forward with his life. He had decided to study social work and help other people with physical disabilities. It was too bad we never saw that happen.

In 2018, I was in Shelton, Washington, at the Mason County Court House office of the assessor. The office was very busy. While I waited, a man entered in an electric wheelchair. He was accompanied by an attendant. I asked the man in the wheelchair if an OT had helped him with his equipment. "You bet she did!" he replied. "She got me all rigged up. Watch this. Get me the phone, please," he said to his attendant. When the attendant secured the phone in a holder on the arm of the chair, the man dialed by saying, "Call my wife." His wife answered her phone. "I'm just calling to show this gal how I can make phone calls," he told her. He disconnected the call. "I'm an insurance salesman. I can make customer calls, submit claims, and other things using this phone and a computer. I can use my eyes and voice to run both the phone and the computer, too. It's amazing. I can support my family thanks to that OT."

I thought of Richard and how he would have loved all the new technology. He would have made a wonderful social worker and may even have gone on to become a professor at a university in Massachusetts.

While writing this story, I contacted Richard's mother. She was surprised to hear from me, and enthusiastically gave me permission to use his real name. In fact, she insisted I use his real name. Judith said she loved talking about Richard again. Judith was proud of Richard and wanted to remember him clearly. Not many people she knew talked about Richard.

Judith also informed me that the social worker at Spaulding Hospital had her fill out paperwork for Medicaid insurance as soon as Richard was admitted to the hospital. So, fortunately, the family had minimal expenses for Richard's care. I was grateful to know that.

Chapter 36

Clint

"Margret, I have a special referral for you," said Susan, a speech therapist,and my supervisor at the Harvard Clinic. "This child has an appointment mid-afternoon on Tuesday."

"I thought I had to be in Braintree on Tuesday," I responded.

"Well, yes, but please leave early to get back here to evaluate Clint. I can't have anyone else see him."

"OK. I'll try my best to be on time." I left the clinic pondering why I had to see this child. I could think of numerous reasons.

On Tuesday, I excused myself from a general occupational therapy staff meeting at Braintree and hurried back to the Harvard clinic. No lunch except a peanut butter and jelly sandwich, which I ate on the drive back. I was rather parched by the time I walked into the clinic. I set up an evaluation room, then greeted the mother, Clint, and his little sister.

For a six-year-old, Clint was not very cordial. He looked at me with suspicion. We left his mother and younger sister in the reception area. During the evaluation, I quickly noted that Clint would be difficult to test using standardized evaluation tools. Clint was non-compliant. I made observations of his gross motor skills.

"How about getting into this swing?" I said with a cheery voice and a smile.

"No."

"OK. How about playing in this ball bath? There are some fun things to find in here."

"No." He folded his arms across his chest.

"OK. Would you like to draw on the chalk board?" Just as I said that, his mother and little sister entered the room.

"No."

"I will," his sister said.

Thinking that I might get some sibling cooperation, I handed his little sister a piece of green colored chalk. Suddenly, Clint bolted out of the treatment room. He ran across the physical therapy gym and out the door to the hall. I ran after him, caught him by the arm just as he was about to run into the parking lot.

I wrestled him back to the children's treatment area, kicking and screaming. I sat down on the floor, holding him from behind with my legs over his legs. My arms held his arms across his chest. He banged his head on my chest while his little sister pummeled my arms and back with her fists. His mother sat in a chair, silently watching the whole thing. It took several minutes before she called her daughter to her side.

Another couple of minutes passed before Clint realized I was not giving into his tantrum. He was getting tired and finally relaxed. "OK. Now that you have calmed down, you need to know that running away is not allowed. When you are here, you will stay in this room until I say you can leave. Do you understand?"

I waited a bit longer before easing my hold of him. He did not answer. "Do you understand?" I repeated.

"Yes," he finally said.

"Now, I'm going to stop holding you and you are going to stand up right here until I tell you what we are going to do. Do you understand?"

"Yes."

"OK." I released my grip on him. He stood up. Then I stood up.

"Now, we are going to draw some pictures at this table. You sit here."

He sat down. I put paper and crayons in front of him. We did a 'Draw-a-Man' picture, then we did "Draw a Picture of Yourself." His picture of himself was of a strong man with big muscles, standing like a superhero with hands on hips.

When they left the clinic, I called the doctor who referred this youngster and told him what happened. I asked for more information. "Why was Clint referred?" I asked.

"This family is in grave danger," the doctor said. "Did the mother do anything to intervene?"

"No. She sat there like she didn't know what to do."

"Exactly," the doctor said. "She is letting the kids do anything they want. Her husband travels extensively. When he comes home, the house is a mess, the kids are wild and won't obey. That little boy is trying to be the man in the family and has no support for being a child. He's very demanding at school. I see he's having severe behavior problems because he won't take direction. I have referred the mother for mental health treatment, but so far nothing has happened to change her parenting behaviors. All I'm asking is for you to help Clint be a child."

"That's a pretty tall order for infrequent visits. Have you referred him to the school for behavior issues there? Is his mother in therapy, or parenting classes?" I asked.

"I referred her for psychiatric treatment, but so far she refused to go. We may have to do an involuntary commitment. Her husband is still considering that. As for our little patient, the school will not be able to get him into counseling until fall."

"I'll see what I can do," I said and ended the conversation. I did not tell the doctor that I would be leaving the clinic in August. I had accepted an instructor position at Worcester State College (now Worcester State University). I was anxious to return to the classroom and teach.

Clint seemed to realize that he was not in control during his therapy time. We got to the point that he accepted my direction, selection of toys, activities, and the sequence of therapy. During our last session his father accompanied Clint. It was the first time I met him. "My wife has finally gotten into treatment. She's actually in the hospital for six weeks," he told me as we entered the therapy room.

"Oh, that's good. I sure hope she gets the help she needs," I said. I explained how Clint and I worked together. "I'm beginning to give him a choice between two activities now. He needs to know that he has some control, but he's not running the show. It's a strategy you can give him at home, too."

We proceeded through the session. Toward the end, Clint balked and refused to make choices between the two things I gave him. "You're to sit in that chair, until you're ready to work," I said. He obeyed. That surprised even me.

I also dimmed the lights. I sat next to his father and we talked for a bit.

When I looked at Clint, he appeared more relaxed. "OK, let's get back to work. You can walk on the balance beam, or you can roll this log by using your feet," I told him. I wanted him to roll the therapy log, but I didn't tell him that. I was giving him a choice. I was on my knees between the balance beam and the therapy tube. Clint walked over to the therapy tube and pointed to it.

"Good choice!" I grinned. At the end of the session, I told Clint that I would not be there next time he came.

"Where are you going?" Clint asked.

"I'm going to teach some people to do what we do here," I answered.

"Can I hug you?" Clint asked.

I was totally surprised by that and teared up immediately. "Oh, yes you can!"

We hugged tightly. "Bye, Clint. You mind your Daddy, OK?"

"OK." He and his father walked out of the clinic. I turned to wipe down some equipment and my tearing eyes.

Chapter 37

Another Surprise

Susan asked, "Would you mind going to lunch with me tomorrow?"

"I think I could do that. So far, I don't have to go anyplace. I'll work with clients until noon, then no one until 2 p.m."

"I've got a meeting in Braintree, but I should be back by 11:30. See you tomorrow." She left me wondering about what tomorrow's lunch topic was. Susan and I had disagreements about several things, primarily administrative policies. We shared some clients and co-treated on several occasion. She was about twenty years younger. I thought she was a good speech therapist. I didn't know her very well as a person, however. We had never eaten lunch together before, so I was a bit perplexed by her sudden request. She knew that I was leaving the following week.

Susan and I met at a charming little restaurant just down on the corner from the clinic. We ordered lunch. "I wanted to meet with you for a couple of reasons," Susan began. "First, I want you to know that I will be leaving a week after you do. I'm going to England. I have a job there and will also take classes."

"Oh, that's a surprise," I said, sipping my coffee. "How long will you be gone?"

"I don't exactly know yet, but probably a couple of years. I want to travel. I've always wanted to see Europe and can do quite a bit on weekends."

"That's exciting. I've never been out of this country, except to Canada."

"The other thing I wanted to talk about is how stubborn you are, and your attitude toward authority."

"Well, yes. I know I can be stubborn, especially when I believe a policy is wrong. I hope you never thought I was angry with you, though. I think you're a very nice person and a good therapist."

"I did at first, but then I came to realize that it wasn't me you were angry with. The past several months in my management role, I came to understand that you have been right about a lot of things." She took a bite of her salad.

I sat a bit stunned. I didn't say anything. I knew she wanted to share something more.

"My meeting at Braintree this morning confirmed that you have been right all along about some of the HealthSouth policies that you refused to use. I can't share exactly what happened, but I was so glad to be turning in my resignation. I'm also glad to be leaving the country. I think I'll learn a lot in a different healthcare environment. I don't want to think about money every time I turn around. I will be able to focus on the patient, which is what I've seen you do time and time again."

"Thank you. That means a lot," I said.

"We probably won't ever have the opportunity to work together again, but I do hope you will think of me as a friend."

"I can do that," I said. "Hate to say it, but it's time for me to get to work. Best of luck on your new adventure." I paid my bill and left to set up the treatment room for my next client.

Chapter 38

Worcester State

I began teaching at Worcester State College (now Worcester State University) in August 1998. I was delighted to be back on a campus teaching hopeful occupational therapy students. At that time, the Occupational Therapy Department was in the process of developing a master's degree in O. T. I would teach an Introduction to Occupational Therapy course in the master of science program. I would also teach a class in pediatrics and therapeutic reasoning using craft techniques. Therapeutic reasoning covers both patients with physical disabilities and patients with psychiatric issues.

In the undergraduate therapeutic reasoning class, students gathered in small groups. All the students were from the New England states, and I was still getting used to the regional culture and expectations. When I introduced myself to classes, I mentioned I was from Washington. Then added, "Washington State." Some of the students would nod their heads as though to say, "That explains her accent." I sounded different from my students. I never thought I had an accent because I spoke pretty much the way people talk on TV or the radio. I also found certain expressions that are not familiar to people in different areas of the country. An example is I refer to carbonated beverages as "pop," in most other areas of the country, those drinks are called "soda."

I discussed cultural differences within the United States during an in-service for parents of children in an early intervention program. One of the mothers insisted that she did not have a "culture." I started to disagree with her. I soon realized that nothing I could say would convince her otherwise. Perhaps she had not traveled to other areas.

There are also some expressions we use that imply that many of us have difficulty identifying individuals from other parts of the world. One of these is, "All Chinese look alike." I brought this up during one of the graduate classes when we were talking about working with people from different ethnicities and cultures. A woman from China was in the class. Before my lecture, I had discussed with her whether she would be upset with what I was going to say.

"No," she answered. "Because we say 'all white people look alike'. Do you mind if I say that?"

"Not at all," I chuckled. "I think that would make a point for the other students."

I started the lecture focusing on working with people from different cultures by recounting my experience with Mexican children in New Mexico, some of whom did not speak English. I also mentioned that growing up in Washington State not far from several Indigenous tribes, some of us had difficulty relating to those who grew up on reservations. Then I said that we used to say, "All Chinese look alike." Immediately, the students looked at our one Chinese student and seemed embarrassed that I would even say such a thing. Then she giggled and said, "We say that 'all white people look alike'." Everyone seemed a bit shocked at first, then we all laughed.

In the spring of 1999, I was informed by Dr. Donna that the faculty was looking to replace me. I was disappointed not to be returning in the fall. The reason they were letting me go was that I did not have a doctorate, and with their program beginning the master of arts program, they wanted all their faculty to have doctorates. The American Occupational Therapy Association was working to move all OTs up to the doctorates.

The Physical Therapists had moved to that advanced degree. I began looking for another job.

At the end of July 1999, I received a call from Dr. Donna inviting me to return. They had not found anyone to hire and wanted me back after all. Although I was a bit reluctant, I overcame my hesitation and said, "Yes."

I had been working at an Early Intervention Program during the summer, and when I quit that job, the director told me she would never hire me again. "If I'd known you were going to go back to the college, I never would have hired you in the first place," she said.

"I'm sorry, but I want to teach," I replied. I felt badly, but not badly enough to say "No" to returning to the teaching position.

Along with the classes I taught the previous year, Dr. Donna asked me to join an interdisciplinary campus committee, which developed writing as a means of learning. I put together a syllabus for a class I had long thought about teaching. I was sure the information would be valuable.

The class would use books written by authors who either had some form of disability, or who knew stories about people with disabilities. The reading list included books by Oliver Sacks, MD, Temple Granden, PhD, and Joni Erikson Tada. Part of the learning experience included visiting the mall in downtown Worcester and pretending to have a disability. The acting student would begin their experiment in a wheelchair. The final exam consisted of a reflection paper as well as a small group presentation about their mall learning experience.

Nine students took the first class. One was a premed student, five were nursing students, two were occupational therapy students, and one was a liberal arts student. The premed student was a challenge for me. He was always questioning why we needed to read something, or why we needed to discuss a particular topic. My lectures revolved around a variety of disabilities and how people learned to cope. The stages of emotional grief individuals go through when faced with trauma or a diagnosis change a life. In fact, those diagnoses also change family life, too.

During our trip to the mall, students were given specific instructions. We went to the mall in the early evening around 5 p. m.. There were wheelchairs at the mall for the students to use. As they split up into their teams, each team was instructed to use the bathroom and determine how accessible it was. Students were also assigned to go into a store and ask for some kind of help. Each student was to have some time in the wheelchair.

When they finished, we met at the food court and ate pizza while we discussed their experiences. The premed student said, "I have never been ignored in my life! I was ignored by the salesperson in the sporting goods store. That had never happened to me before. What an eye-opener!"

"How did that make you feel?" I asked.

"I'm not sure, but I think I was kind of angry. I was frustrated, too."

"Do you think that might help you have some empathy for those with handicaps?"

"Oh, definitely!" he responded.

Other students had similar responses.

"I couldn't believe how hard it was to get into the bathroom with that wheelchair," one of the nursing students said. "Even with someone holding the door open for me."

We talked more about the experiences and continued talking until we realized that the mall was closing, and we had to leave. I was delighted to have provided them with an eye-opening experience assignment.

When the final class arrived the feedback I received was positive. The premed student stated he finally understood better what his grandfather was going through. The information he gained made him more patient with his grandfather who suffered from Parkinson's disease. I felt the class had been worth it if only for his attitude change.

Worcester State had hired a woman with a doctorate. And another faculty member was accepted to the University of Massachusetts graduate school to work on her doctorate. Perhaps my fate had been in the stars all along. Everett accepted another job and we were going to move again.

Chapter 39

Maryland 2000

On June 21, 2000, we signed paperwork selling the house in Bolton, Massachusetts, and left for Maryland. I was turning 60. I still wanted to write, but I needed a job as well. I wasn't ready to retire, nor was I willing to give up the dream of getting a doctorate and teaching in another O. T. program.

We found a house in Upper Marlboro, Maryland, just a couple of miles from Washington, D.C. I set out looking for a job. No occupational therapy jobs were advertised, but I saw a job for a kindergarten teacher in Prince George's County School District. Since I had a master's degree in early childhood special education, I decided to apply.

What a huge mistake! I do well with young children individually or in small groups of two or three, but the class I tried teaching had 27 children ranging in age from nearly four years to nearly seven years old. Their I.Q.s likely ranged anywhere from low 60s to over 150. In addition, a couple of children were mainstreamed with Individual Education Plans (IEPs). It was the beginning of all-day kindergarten for the district. Because there were few aides in the district, I had no help in the classroom.

I drove home crying almost every night. I couldn't believe how I treated the children. I had no discipline with all of those children. I did have lesson plans. No matter how I began the day, my classroom descended into chaos. In no time at all I was yelling at children to sit down and be quiet. It seemed that I was always angry at them for some reason or another. The only somewhat enjoyable times were story time right after lunch and the minutes we waited for buses at the end of the day.

Soon after I began work as a kindergarten teacher, my father-in-law was diagnosed with terminal cancer. Mr. Kingrey lived in Virginia, a three-hour drive from our home. We traveled to see how we could help him. He had a friend living with him, and he decided that we were not needed. My father-in-law refused to go to the hospital when necessary. He insisted that once the chemotherapy port was in, he would recover. His sister and stepfather lived nearby and could help, if necessary, he told us. We drove back to Maryland to await a phone call.

I abhor lying and work very hard to never tell untruths. However, after receiving a phone call from one mother asking why her daughter was crying when she had to come to school, I decided, for my sake and for the sake of the children, to out-and-out lie.

It was true that my father-in-law had terminal cancer, but I told the principal of the school that I needed to go to Virginia to help care for him. I would have to quit my teaching job. The principal was very upset with me, as well he should have been. The district was so short of teachers that he told me he would replace me with a teacher's aide instead of a qualified teacher. I reminded him that even though I had a master's degree in early childhood special education, I had never worked in a classroom as a teacher. I was not a certified teacher, which he knew when he hired me. He decided to allow me to break my contract for the rest of the school year.

Everett and I traveled to Virginia every other weekend for the next two months. I did not help my father-in-law; in fact, he told me I irritated him. But Everett was glad I was there by his side, and I was glad to be with him as well. On November 1, 2000, Everett's father passed away. We travelled to Virginia for the funeral. We did not stay long because Everett needed to return to work and finish a critical project.

A few weeks later, we returned to Virginia to help clear out his father's home and help his aunt settle the estate. The house was sold, and our trips to Virginia dwindled the remainder of the time we lived in Maryland.

Chapter 40

Returning to Occupational Therapy Work

In December I saw an advertisement for a part-time occupational therapy position with the Prince George's County School District. I decided to apply. The job would entail traveling among several schools. The schools covered a large area just outside of Washington D.C. The district office for special education was in Hyattsville, Maryland. I was hired. On the days I worked, I checked in at the district office, then drove to one or two schools during the day, three days a week. This job gave me time at home two days a week. Returning to my life as an occupational therapist was comforting, especially after trying to teach kindergarten.

Back in the middle of the1960s, I volunteered in a school occupied by mostly black students and teachers in Corpus Christi, Texas. I was not an occupational therapist then. Now I was working in schools that were filled with students and teachers who were all Black. Their families had been in this country for generations. I was a little out of my depth. I faced new, unfamiliar cultural differences, nothing like what I had been taught at Worcester State College. In Maryland, I was challenged in a completely different way to understand the students, teachers and families. I tried to look at everything from their perspective. I am empathetic toward other cultures and did my best to adjust.

The Supervisor of Occupational Therapy told me to strictly adhere to the department evaluation process. She saw to it that I was trained by one of the other O.T.s. We could use other test procedures; however, at the beginning of every new evaluation we began with their strict internal process.

Their evaluation featured clinical observations that A. Jean Ayres, PhD, OTR, developed as part of the Sensory Integration testing. We could also use the Draw-A-Man Test, the Buriniks-Oseretsky Test of Motor Development, and the Winterhaven Perceptual Test. The Supervisor of Occupational Therapy preferred that we report on each individual child to her before using other tests. She preferred that we have tests with numerical, statistically relevant data on the children. Then, if deeper research was needed, the first data could be used for test–retest purposes. I understood her perspective and tried to comply with the department's standards.

I later learned that another reason she required us to be so compliant with her requirements was that some of these tests were not standardized on any black students. In addition, the school district was using a research tool to gather more data on this population.

Chapter 41

A Remarkable Year 2001

The first few months working for the Prince George's County School District went well. With a couple of weekdays free, I began writing. I enjoyed being out and about during the workdays. In June I read that Towson University's Occupational Science doctorate program was open for applications. Everett and I discussed the possibility of my going back to school to earn a doctorate. I wrestled with the idea for a couple of months. Finally, I called the Occupational Science Department at Towson in Towson, Maryland, to talk to Dr. Reitz, the head of the OT School at Towson. In August 2001, I drove the fifty miles up to Towson with my resume in hand for an appointment with Dr. Reitz.

When I arrived and checked in with the secretary, she showed me into a conference room. I sat there for nearly an hour. I was about to leave when Dr. Reitz entered the room. She apologized for the long wait. She had an emergency to attend to. I introduced myself and stated the purpose of my visit while she looked over my resume.

"Excuse me. Can you wait a bit longer?" she said.

"Yes," I said. I had no other appointments and since it was still early, I didn't worry about rush hour traffic piling up on the interstate. I just wished I had brought a book.

When Dr. Reitz returned, she asked, "Could you teach for us? I have a faculty member who must take a medical leave of absence. We need someone to teach at least two courses this semester: one in therapeutic activities and also the Introduction to Occupational Therapy for the Master's Program. As faculty, you can take a course in the doctoral program."

It seems that I had walked into the department at just the right time to fill their needs, combined with my own desire to teach and earn a doctorate. Dr. Reitz further explained she was late for our meeting because she had been talking with their Fieldwork Coordinator, who had just been diagnosed with cancer. Dr. Reitz was caught by surprise. The Fieldwork Coordinator was unexpectedly scheduled for surgery, then chemotherapy. Also, her husband had recently died. They would not have time to advertise the position before September classes began.

I offered to take the position immediately.

"Good," Dr. Reitz said. She added that the secretary would give me the paperwork and I should fill it out before I left.

I got the paperwork from the secretary and filled it out. After returning it to the secretary, Dr. Reitz reviewed the faculty orientation schedule. She even gave me a faculty parking lot card to put on my dashboard. "I'll give you keys and other things at orientate on." I would be at Towson University two days a week. The graduate class was in the evening on one of those days.

I let my supervisor at the Prince George's School District know that I would be attending class on Tuesday evenings for three hours at Towson. With the long drive home, I asked if I could work Tuesday and Thursday, with Wednesday off to recover from the late night on Tuesday. I would also be teaching classes on Monday and Friday at Towson. All this began in September 2001. I was getting settled into the routine, and dealing with short sleep cycles, when tragedy struck.

Chapter 42

Scary Things Happen

Tuesday morning of September 11, 2001, I walked into the special education classroom. Eight children who were diagnosed with either autism or mental retardation sat on the floor. There was no teacher in the classroom, only one aide. The TV was on and as I glanced at the screen I saw a plane fly into a tall building.

"Why are you showing this terrible movie to these children at this time of day?" I chided the aide.

"This is no movie. This is happening right now in New York," she retorted. "Didn't you hear the news?"

Fortunately, the TV was muted. We stood and watched for a few minutes, stunned. I asked about the teacher. "He's with the principal. The school district hasn't decided what we're going to do yet."

"I don't know what I'm supposed to do either. I had better return to the special education department and find out."

I drove to Hyattsville, which is closer to the D.C. area and closer to the Pentagon. I turned the car radio on and heard that a plane had crashed into the Pentagon. As I parked the car, I saw smoke rising into the air. I walked into the Occupational Therapy Department.

"Do you know what I'm supposed to be doing?" I asked the secretary.

"No, Sarah is out and none of the other therapists are here."

We listened to the radio for thirty minutes. Another plane had gone down in Pennsylvania. The phone rang. The secretary answered it. She turned to me with a look of shock. "The superintendent decided to close all the schools. Kids will be bused home as soon as possible. You may as well go home, too."

One of the other O.T.s walked into the office and said she had talked to Sarah. We were all to go home. No one would be allowed into the D.C. area. All roads were being used to evacuate. I thought immediately about my husband whose office was in a tall building near the Pentagon, but on the Maryland side of the dividing line. I needed to check on him. As I drove to his office via some back roads, I watched police putting up barricades on the westbound highway lanes. Inadvertently, I drove through a red light. I had never done that in my life. When I arrived at Everett's office, I rang the buzzer to be let in. No one came to the door. His truck was in the parking lot, so I knew he hadn't left. I phoned his cell phone. No answer. I pounded on the door, still no one came to let me in. I went back downstairs to my car and drove home.

As soon as I walked into the house, I turned on the TV and once again sat stunned. All airline flights were cancelled. Occasional jets flew overhead, but we were not that far from Andrews Air Force Base outside of Washington, D.C. The jets I heard were from the Air Force base. When Everett finally came home for dinner, he said everyone in the office was watching the flames and smoke from the Pentagon through an office window at the back of their building. They did not hear me knocking on the door, nor did they hear the buzzer. He had left his cell phone on his desk and hadn't heard it either.

Everett was still on inactive reserve status with the Air Force, so he decided to check his uniform and other military equipment in case he was called back into service.

I continued to watch the news on TV. Fortunately, Everett was never called up to active duty. School was cancelled everywhere for the next few days. Classes at Towson were also cancelled. There was time to talk to neighbors, some of whom worked in Washington, D.C. and were home. The following Monday, we all returned to work as usual, although it was no longer "as usual".

Often conversations began with, "Where were you when the Pentagon was hit . . .?" Stories were shared as we all tried to cope with the possibility of another attack.

At roughly the same time, anthrax was discovered in some mailboxes in our neighborhood and in Washinton, D.C. One of our neighbors abandoned the mail in his mailbox. The mail carrier on our street asked if the gentleman was OK. I said that I saw him working in his yard over the weekend, so I assumed he was.

I walked down the block and talked to him. He said he was terrified to touch his mail. He said he worked in a top-secret government facility, although he did not say which one. "I can get some gloves and help you go through your mail, if you want," I told him.

"Oh, I'll stop on my way home tomorrow and get gloves and a respirator then get my mail," he replied. I saw him a few days later. He told me there wasn't anything in his mail to worry about after all. He was overreacting. Or was he?

In October 2001, a sniper shot a woman and a man at a gas station. Then another shooting happened at a school in Prince George's County School District. A woman had been in line to drop off her nephew at a school near Washington, D.C. The youngster got out of the car. As he walked along the sidewalk shots were fired from a wooded area across from the school. Her nephew was hit. The woman was a nurse. She pulled her nephew back into the car and rushed him to the hospital where she worked. The child survived. Thank God. All across the area schools were locked down. It was scary.

And yet my therapies continued. The routine was for me to park in the staff parking lot which was usually at the back of the school. I would lug my therapy equipment into the school through a back door. Now with the schools locked, I parked in the staff parking lot, lugged my equipment around the building to the front door, and buzzed a buzzer until someone came to open the door. Most of the schools were not equipped with buttons at the office where the door could be unlocked from inside. I stood outside waiting for someone to open the door. That was a bit uncomfortable, as I didn't know who might be hiding across from the front of the building ready to shoot.

Police cautioned everyone to be on the lookout for a white van reported near one of the shootings. One day when I came out of a school, I noticed that the tire on the front driver's side of my car was low. I stopped at an auto shop not too far away to have the mechanic check the tire. "Could you drive around to the back of the shop?" the mechanic asked after I told him what I needed.

"Sure." I drove around to the back away from the main street.

"With that sniper out there, I didn't want us near the street while I checked your tire." He checked the tire pressure and told me it had a puncture somewhere. He'd have to take the tire off to repair it, or I could buy a new tire and be on my way. I decided to buy a new tire as I didn't want a patch job failing during that long commute to Towson, or between schools either.

It was several weeks before the shooter was finally apprehended in a blue sedan. Once more, I could travel between the schools without worry. Just as a precaution, schools were kept on lockdown for another two weeks.

Chapter 43

Busy Schedule 2002

In January 2002, I started taking two classes at Towson, teaching two classes and working two days a week at Prince George's Public School District.

One day while at Towson not too long into the new semester, Nancy Blake, an OT and professor, whose class I took over in the Fall semester of 2001 stopped by my office. She asked how things were going. I said, "Pretty well, except for the commute. I'm just very tired."

"Why don't you stay at my house? I have an extra bedroom now and I'd love to have you there. Another student lives with me, and we do Bible study one evening a week. I think you'd like it." Nancy was nearly done with her chemotherapy. She said she needed company. After talking about the option over with Everett, I began staying at Nancy's house two nights a week. That was a big help in reducing my fatigue. It provided fun and companionship for all three of us.

I juggled the schedule at the school district. I stayed in Towson overnight on Sunday and Monday nights. I drove home after class on Tuesday night to work at the District on Wednesday and Thursday. That allowed me to study and do the usual housework and grocery shopping on Friday, Saturday, and Sunday. With a little more sleep and a lighter schedule, I started to write a book about my life in Alaska from 1986 to 1989.

Nancy's home was on a spacious couple of acres. It included a large garden, a barn, but no animals, and some very large black maple trees. The upstairs bedroom where I slept was cozy, but sometimes cold. Nancy provided additional blankets for freezing nights. We usually had a quick breakfast together, then I headed to the university.

Everett was busy with work. The small company where he worked was bought by a larger defense-industry company. He helped develop some interesting antenna designs and did testing. However, the new company owners did not seem to understand the complexities of his work. Again, Everett faced a dilemma. He was not sure how long his job would last under the new management. He cast a wide net and began exploring his options.

I was up to my eyebrows in studying, work, and trying to stay abreast of changes in the occupational therapy profession. With that in mind, I decided to attend the National American Occupational Therapy Association (AOTA) Conference in Philadelphia in April. Everett would go along for the ride. He didn't like the idea of my being in Philly without an escort. Attending any National AOTA conference always energized me.

One afternoon I was sitting near a corridor at the conference center waiting for the next session to begin. A young woman ran over to me with a big smile. "Hi. Do you remember me?" she asked.

After staring at her for a moment, I realized she had been one of my students at Worcester State, but as usual, I didn't recall her name.

"I'm Amanda. You taught me how to sew on a button! Thank you. I've needed that skill so many times and I always think of you."

"Oh, yes, now I remember. That was 'special training' in my office. I'm so glad it has been helpful!" We chatted a bit more. She was now married and the mother of one child. She worked as an occupational therapist in Massachusetts. Amanda said she loved her career and was so glad she had become an occupational therapist. "I'm sorry you didn't stay at Worcester State."

"Well, my husband changed jobs and I thought I'd better go with him," I laughed. I told her that I was currently working for a school district, teaching at Towson, and working on my doctorate in occupational science.

It was time for the next session to begin. We said a cordial goodbye. Amanda hurried off to join her colleagues. I wandered into the next session, reminiscing about Massachusetts and the experiences I had there.

Returning from the conference, I began to reflect on my own patterns. It was time to jump back into my hectic schedule. I wasn't sure how long I could keep up the pace. After all, I was soon to be sixty-one years old. Was getting a doctorate going to be worth it? I still wanted to write, too, and there was little time to spend on my Alaska book.

Chapter 44

A Vacation in 2002

When Everett came home one night in May, he told me we were going to the John C. Campbell Folk School for a week. I was totally amazed. I had not seen him so excited about anything, ever. He was making some changes. In the early spring, he started doing some wood turning in his spare time. Someone told him about the John C. Campbell Folk School in Brasstown, North Carolina, and the classes they had. A world-class wood turner from Norway would teach a class there in June.

"You need to get online and see what you can take. We're going." I looked at the school's website and saw a class in Swedish knitting. It was being taught by a woman from Texas. A whole week of knitting, listening to music, eating home-grown food that I didn't grow and didn't cook, and meeting new people. That was right up my alley. The history of the school on their website was fascinating. I could even write an article for *ADVANCE for Occupational Therapy.*

I contacted the editor of *ADVANCE.* She wrote back, saying she would be interested in an article. After all, the John C. Campbell Folk School was doing what O.T. used to do many years ago. They taught local people crafts that could be used in their daily lives, not just for hobbies, but also for earning a bit of income. Specialized cooking and gardening were taught there as well.

We left in June for a week. I had already contacted the director of the folk school to ask if I could interview him and any willing attendees. The director was very obliging, even though he was relatively new to the job. He also told me that there was a woman who lived on the school grounds who had been an occupational therapist during the Depression. They would celebrate her 100th birthday soon. He suggested I might want to interview her also. How fortunate for me to be able to get her story, too!

A couple from Massachusetts started the folk school in the early 20th Century. They wanted Southern Appalachia people to relearn skills that could sustain them during difficult times. Skills in gardening, basket making, woodworking, horseshoeing, and so on were featured for anyone wanting to attend. The founders' ideas fit so nicely into the philosophy of occupational therapy. We all need skills, not just to "keep busy while convalescing," but to develop real occupations necessary for a meaningful life.

In the Swedish knitting class, there were fifteen women from various states. We all had different occupations. Everett's class appealed mostly to men who had been woodworkers for a long time. They were there to gain more skill and learn new techniques. Interestingly, my mother was of Swedish heritage, a first-born generation in America. Everett's mother was of Norwegian heritage. We both felt that we were connecting in some way to our ancestry.

The week progressed quickly, with meals served in a large dining room. Everyone was assigned a table so we could get to know each other during the entire week. In the evening, we enjoyed musical performances and demonstrations from other classes. Toward the end of the week, I hurried off to talk with the school director. We met on the porch of the original school building that had just been remodeled. He had given me some information earlier to read so that I could focus my questions on a deeper level.

He took me to the home of the 100-year-old woman who was an OT so I could meet her "officially". She was visually impaired, but still able to live in her own home. The school provided her meals. "I still make my own breakfast, including coffee," she told me proudly.

"Let's sit out here in the sunshine where we can stay warm." She gestured toward a small deck beside the kitchen. "I can never get enough sun these days."

Mrs. Myres began telling me that she went to OT school in the early 1930s in Massachusetts. Then she was hired at Walter Reed Army Hospital in Washington, D.C. She worked there for just a couple of years. Like many other people around the country, Mrs. Myres was laid off because of the Depression. She traveled to North Carolina to the John C. Campbell Folk School to teach blind people how to knit. When she was contacted to come back to work at Walter Reed, she decided to stay at the Folk School. By then she had fallen in love and was about to be married. She worked at the Folk School the rest of her professional life.

Mrs. Myres helped expand the school, taught multiple classes, and raised her family nearby. Her husband passed away in his mid-sixties. She stayed on at the Folk School and only recently quit teaching because of her failing eyesight. Mrs. Myres showed me several of her current projects. She grew some of her own produce. Some plants were in pots on the porch surrounding us during the interview. What an inspiration she was! I saw how the underlying foundation of her training as an occupational therapist impacted her own life. As she said, "I learned how to live my life through the years, based on what I learned in O. T. School, and what I taught my students. One of the most valuable things they taught me was to be persistent."

Everett took several pictures of the gardens, the blacksmith shop, and the wood-fired ceramics kiln. On the way back home to Maryland, I pondered how I was going to logically include the interviews into the story of the Folk School. I called the editor of *ADVANCE* to get her advice. She directed me to write the article based on the Folk School, and include the interview with Mrs. Myres as a side-bar. I had learned enough about writing articles by then to understand what she meant. The article was published in *ADVANCE* in the Fall of 2002.

Chapter 45

Back to Work and School

The Fall Semester at Towson included a course in statistics as well as one elective. I decided to venture over to the English Department and take a graduate class in writing as my elective. As for the statistics class, I didn't care how many times I would take the class, because unless I used statistics every day, I forgot the concepts as soon as I left the classroom. Formula's were not my strong suit at all. Fortunately, my fellow students helped me remember some things well enough to pass the tests.

One day, just over halfway through the semester, the professor came into the room with a frown on his face. "I have never taught a class where there were more worries!" he said as he stood in front of us. "I have had more of you in my office concerned about your grade than I ever have had before, and there aren't that many of you in this class. Let me reassure you, none of you are going to fail." He then went on to lecture about another obscure concept with a formula.

When we left the class, we started talking about what he had said at the beginning of class. The professor walked by and again said, "You aren't going to fail the class. You O.T.s are a bunch of worriers." One of the students replied, "Well, we're expected to be perfect. We work with people. We don't like making mistakes."

"Statistics isn't an exact science. It only gives you a reasonable estimate. So quit worrying, at least in my class anyway," he responded as he walked away. At the end of the semester, we compared grades. We had all gotten an "A" in statistics. I probably wouldn't have passed if it hadn't been for the help of two of my classmates who were much better at inputting numbers into the computer program than I was. They proofread my work and guided my understanding of the statistics program's formulas.

Chapter 46

Another aspect of OT

One of my fellow students asked me to come visit her at her workplace. Her job was at the Children's Division of the National Institutes of Health in Bethesda, Maryland. Penny had been an O.T. longer than I had, but she opted to do something very different from clinical work. I was curious, so I said, "Yes!"

"Okay. How about next Tuesday?" I said.

"That would be great. Come about ten a.m., and I'll introduce you to the head of the department, give you a tour, and maybe you can even sit in on a grant funding presentation."

On Tuesday, I arrived at the agreed-upon hour. Penny told me the presentation was first. I was just there as an observer, which meant that I needed to keep my mouth shut. Penny was always very polite, but I got the drift. Watching the presentation of the proposed research project, I realized this person had probably been on the faculty at UNC Chapel Hill when my friend from the Children's Therapy Unit was going to school there for her master's degree. Maybe she had him as a teacher. I jotted down his name to ask her.

When the presentation finished, Penny and I went for lunch. "I think my boss will be available to meet you when we get back," she said. "You know, I've asked any number of our colleagues to come visit me where I work, but you're the only one who has ever shown up."

"I'm glad I came. It's interesting to see how various people use their O.T. education. I can certainly see how your background in pediatrics gives you the knowledge to help guide research and improve funding."

Penny introduced me to her boss, then left me to go catch up on her own work. I chatted with the head of the department for a short time. I asked why children with autism were not included in the research proposal. More research needed to be done in that area.

"Evidently, we did not think of that. Thank you. I will ask him about doing that. Maybe he can tweak this study to include autism. We are seeing more children diagnosed with autism and if the trend continues, it's going to be a large issue for schools. He comes to D.C. frequently with proposals and they almost never get turned down. He'd be a good one to advance that research."

I went to find Penny to let her know I was leaving. She walked me to my car, then returned to work. On the way home, I thought about how people who fund research seemed to be isolated from my everyday world. There needed to be more communication between those of us in clinics and schools, and those in government. A tighter relationship would enhance realistic research goals. We all needed more collaboration among the various groups in O.T. and the government.

We were asked early in our doctorate program what kind of research we wanted to perform for our doctorate degrees. I knew I wanted to do something about occupational therapy and writing, but I had no clue just how. I was getting closer to formulating an outline of my own ideas.

Chapter 47

Busy Again Spring 2003

In the Spring of 2003, I joined a writing group at the Senior Center in Bowie, Maryland. It was close to Upper Marlboro, so it would be an easy drive. There was a deli in Bowie where I liked to meet with a friend. She was a clinical psychologist who worked in schools and was also a writer.

The Prince Georges County School District was experiencing some changes. I was asked to serve yet another school. The district was still short-staffed. I was assigned to assess one child who had severe tantrums. Frankie hit one teacher, giving her a black eye. I went to observe Frankie in the classroom. After seeing him work on the blackboard, I thought an evaluation was in order. Frankie kept switching hands as he wrote, never crossing his midline. We already had permission from the parents to test him.

Frankie and I went into a small room to begin the formal testing. He refused to sit in the chair next to me. He wandered around the room. When I tried to coax him to sit down, he got more agitated. I decided to let the situation rest and try again in a couple of days.

The next time I tried to test Frankie, he participated only for a short time before getting up and moving about the room. It was time for recess, so I walked with him to the playground. He ran off to the far side of the playground, where he started kicking at the fence. "He's a piece of work," one of the teachers said as I turned to leave.

"Does he do that often?" I asked.

"Oh, yeah. We have to really watch him, too, or he'll start beating on another kid," she told me.

Gosh. I needed to discuss Frankie with my supervisor. With his behavioral issues, I would not be able to use the protocol the district demanded. Although I tried to talk to Sarah about this child, she was out on leave for several weeks. I decided I would have to do what I had to do. Again I used clinical observations and as much of the formal test as I could obtain. I also took time to interview Frankie's mother. Then I wrote the report. It was a gamble. At the parent conference, I recommended that this youngster receive some behavior management in the classroom. In addition, I recommended that he have a child psychological evaluation.

I made an appointment with Sarah, who was now back from her leave. When I walked into the room, Sarah said, "I'm glad you wanted this meeting. I have been meaning to talk with you. You remember Frankie, that youngster you evaluated a couple of months ago?"

"Yes," I replied, knowing full well what was coming. My testing and report were incomplete and not up to school district standards.

"We went to a meeting with the therapists at the Children's Hospital Mental Health Unit. They reviewed their findings, and showed us your report on Frankie. Every once in a while Children's writes the same kind of report you submitted. When they do, we always criticize them for being too vague and unsubstantiated. I was really embarrassed. I wish you had asked another therapist to evaluate that child. A second opinion would have strengthened your findings."

"Sometimes kids just don't fit our mold. You were not available and everyone else was too busy." I was a bit defensive, but I kept my voice down.

"Well, nonetheless, you could have waited."

"I'm sorry if I made you uncomfortable."

"So, what did you want to talk to me about?" Sarah asked.

"I wanted to give you this personally. I'm leaving the school district to teach and work on my doctorate. And I am finishing a book." I handed her the resignation letter.

"We'll hate to lose you, but I can understand. If that's what you want."

We left the room, but the tension between us was still there.

I had a few weeks more at Prince Georges County Schools. During that time, I was able to enjoy being out in the district. In one classroom, I had been working with all the children. The teacher, teacher's aide, and I decided that we all wanted to arrange a Mother's Day lunch. The children would prepare most of the food, serve it, and give their mothers a small gift that they made at school.

We set the tables with tablecloths, positioned the silverware from the cafeteria, and arranged the glassware. We even made ice cream using two old crank ice cream makers. One was Everett's and mine, the other one we borrowed from another teacher. The students wrote invitations. They were mailed to each mother or grandmother. It was a fun event. Some of the mothers had never been celebrated in quite that way before. They were amazed at how well their seven-and eight-year-old learning-disabled children participated.

After the mothers and grandmothers left, we got busy cleaning up from the party. Extra ice cream was sent down to the principal's office, to the counselor, and the secretary. They were happily surprised and enjoyed the treats and recognition.

On my last day, I went to see Frankie. He was not in the classroom when I arrived. The teacher said she had sent him to the office. I walked to the office and saw his mother sitting outside the office door. "Hello, I'm glad to see you."

"Hello. What's going on?" I asked.

"Frankie got into trouble again, and the principal called me. When I arrived, the principal asked me to wait until he'd had time to talk to him first. I wanted you to know, though, that we had Frankie evaluated by a child psychiatrist. He was diagnosed with Childhood Schizophrenia. We will be sending him to the Children's Hospital Mental Health Unit for a while."

"Oh, my gosh. I'm sorry."

"No. I'm glad we finally have a diagnosis. It's not pretty, but I'm glad we finally know what needs to be done," she confided. "Frankie can get some help. He will improve. If it hadn't been for your recommendation, I don't know if we would have gotten him to the right place. You probably don't know that Frankie also has a cousin, a teenager, who has the same diagnosis. That cousin is in juvenile detention for having shot someone. That could have been my son's fate, too. Now, I think we can make some corrections and avoid that."

Just then the bell rang. School was over, and children began heading for the buses. "I am leaving the school district," I told her. "I am teaching at Towson and going to graduate school, too. I overloaded my schedule, and it's just too much. I will not be back here in the fall."

"I'm sorry to hear that, but I understand." We parted company. I was glad I made that referral so Frankie could get the help he needed. A great deal could be done for him.

Chapter 48

June 2003 and Beyond

The American Occupational Therapy Association (AOTA) conference in June 2003 was in Washington, D.C.—not too far from our home. The book in which I had a small story was being sold by SLACK, Inc. at their booth. Dr. Labovitz would also be at the conference signing books. She was an occupational therapist on the faculty at New York University and had requested patient stories several years before. I knew my story would be in the book, so all of us authors were excited to see our stories finally published. I already had a signed copy, which Dr. Labovitz sent to each author a couple of months before the conference I did not need another copy, but I stopped by the SLACK, Inc. booth to see if they wanted authors of stories to sign their stories.

I was told to hang around, but it really wasn't necessary. Someone overheard the conversation and asked me to sign her book. As I turned to go, Dr. Labovitz said she wanted all the authors to meet on the steps of the convention building after the next session. She wanted a picture of as many author/contributors as she could gather. When picture-taking finished, several authors of stories in the book got together and enjoyed filling in backgrounds. It was not too long after that conference that Dr. Labovitz died of cancer. It was very sad for all of us as well as for the profession.

That summer I had little work as an occupational therapist. Unusual for me, and a refreshing change. Instead of OT, however, I worked on my memoir, ALASKA STORIES:

A Memoir. I often sat at the kitchen table after Everett left for work, pondering how to write a book! What was the purpose of writing my story? After reading several books about writing and listening to feedback from some trusted friends I began. Then I stopped. The Fall semester began, and I was back doing something I loved. The book could wait.

At this stage of my life, I dropped clinical work. Instead, I concentrated on teaching and taking classes. I felt that I was beginning a new career at the age of sixty-three. Upon returning to Towson, I was met in the hall one day by a former professor from the University of Puget Sound! He had been on the faculty there when I was a student. My professor and his wife moved to Maryland from Washington State during the summer. It was strange being on the faculty with him and quite a surprise to find myself referring to him as a colleague. We did not see one another often, however. He took over teaching in the therapeutic media lab where I taught my first few semesters at Towson. I was only teaching one class in the fall. That worked out well and gave me more time to study.

I did more than study. I also had time to attend the writer's group at the Bowie Senior Center. Since we would be taking a class in Qualitative Research in the spring of 2004, I asked the woman who started the Bowie Writer's Group if I could interview her and use that session for the research class. She was kind enough to say, "Yes."

Winona was living in her daughter's remodeled basement not far from Bowie. When Winona's husband became ill, they moved into that basement apartment. Both Winona and her husband were on the faculty at a university in New York State. She was on the nursing faculty. As I began the interview, she confided in me that she was born and raised in Oregon. She knew many of the places in Washington State that I wrote about in the writing group. After an hour or so, we completed the first of our sessions which I planned to use for my class.

Each interview was recorded on a tape recorder. I transcribed the recordings into transcripts then analyzed them for themes. Following the analysis, I began consolidating the information into a single case study.

Winona had an early-onset form of multiple sclerosis (MS). She still walked and conducted most of her own activities. However she had a wheelchair in case she needed to use it for longer distances. Winona often used the wheelchair to go from the parking lot into the Bowie Senior Center and back. She no longer could drive herself.

The basement apartment was equipped with an electronic seat to carry her upstairs when she had dinner or did other activities with her daughter's family. Much of the time, however, she prepared her own meals in her apartment and enjoyed reading, writing and watching some television. In fact, we enjoyed the same programs, mostly on public television stations.

After finishing the interviews and transcribing the tapes, I began writing my paper. I struggled with the conclusion. I wrote to make money. My motivation was purely for self-aggrandizement. It was true that I had something worth writing, but I also hoped to gain a modicum of notoriety. Winona's motivation was much more noble. She had written research papers in nursing and public health for many years as a faculty member at Decker School of Nursing, SUNY in Binghamton, New York. She and her husband had also spoken at public health conferences. He was a department head and both were researchers. They guided students' research.

After many discussions, I finally realized that Winona started the writing group at Bowie Senior Center to provide herself and her husband, when he was still alive, a way of meeting other like-minded people. Most of the people in the group were college educated, some had been on faculties and were now retired. One woman was a musicologist and had a fascinating background. She was also a consummate researcher. When we got into a discussion about fraudulent charities, she spent hours looking up the actual percentages of donations for numerous charities that were used to provide the services the charity claimed to have spent on services. Winona found real common ground with the participants in the writers group. She often went to lunch with members of the group also, giving her conversation at a level she could not have with her own grandchildren, or daughter.

During the spring semester of 2004, I realized that I would probably never finish the doctoral program. Not only was I getting older, but there was considerable contention regarding the process of study. Another semester of classes was added to the doctoral program. I was not getting much writing done on the book I had been told by the pastor of my church that I had to finish.

I attended the Episcopal church not far from our home in Maryland when we first moved there. Reverend Martha was my spiritual counselor. We only met once a month. One day she walked into our meeting and asked if I was expecting something from our Lord.

"Not exactly," I replied. "Why do you ask?"

"Well, this morning when I was in the shower, I got a message. I was to tell you to finish your book about Alaska."

"Oh, my goodness. I've been hassling with finding time to work on that and also finishing the paper I'm supposed to write for my qualitative research class. Guess, I'd better get with it!" We talked about several other things and I left, knowing that I had to use my time better.

Everett worked with open eyes, and was again realizing that his company position and the company probably would end soon. The company was not doing well. They were finishing up one contract, but had not secured new contracts. Several of the other engineers left to form a new company of their own. We predicted another year at best in Maryland.

I withdrew from the doctoral program at the end of spring semester, 2004. Besides working on my book and running a couple of critique groups for Maryland Writers' Association, I decided I wanted to enclose the back deck for a sunroom. I envisioned myself sitting out there to read and write at least three-quarters of the year without the bother of mosquitoes or flies. Several deer and many squirrels paraded through our backyard most days as well. It was always fun to watch them. Everett and I hired a contractor and proceeded with the sunroom.

Chapter 49

Can't Seem to Retire

I spent the summer writing, reading and being "retired" from occupational therapy, but I missed the contact with other people in the profession as well as clients. When I saw an advertisement for home health therapists in the area, I applied for a part-time job. After the interview, I learned that I would have to take a month of training to learn the computer system and all the new regulations for Medicare reimbursement. The next training course was not until March, 2005; however, I would be enrolled in that class if I was willing to drive to Arnold. I said I would wait for a course to be offered closer.

With my next job secure, I wrote and enjoyed the Christmas holidays. Everett took time off during the holidays, but he was worried about his next position. He intensified his job search. I predicted we would stay in Maryland. The sunroom was finished.

We explored the Eastern Shore of Maryland. Again, I found a different cultural experience in that part of the state. On the Eastern Shore, many of the families were descendants of original English immigrants. Traditions and long-time expectations were understood by the locals, but not by me. Language included unfamiliar words and phrases. Fishing and crabbing as well as farming were the primary areas of employment. Along the ocean front many summer service jobs supported families. In the winter tourists were few, those jobs disappeared, and people learned to plan for scarcity.

I finally attended the orientation class. Updates seemed long. I was not used to sitting behind a computer all day, nor was I accustomed to complex computer programs. The logic and reason for the steps needed to write reports for Medicare escaped me. Paperwork to submit billing to Medicare, or other insurance companies, was disorderly, in my opinion.

Each state's rules complicated the paperwork. In Maryland, the occupational therapy program was buried within a multiple-step rehabilitation program. Physical therapy overshadowed both speech therapy and occupational therapy—at least that's what I recall. Also, I did not understand why there was no way to evaluate a client and decide that therapy was unnecessary. An evaluation-only option was not evident in the computer program. The computer program always insisted on therapy. I could think of several of instances where I evaluated a client in New Mexico when I did not feel that therapy was necessary. Usually, in those cases, I would instruct either the client, and/or caregiver in what to do to accomplish what the client needed.

Oddly, little or no occupational therapy work came my way from the contract company. I was very surprised, as they told me I probably would be very busy. I waited for referrals. Anyway, I was now busy writing and managing workshops for Maryland Writers' Association. I had started drawing my social Security checks when I turned sixty-two. According to federal rule, I could only earn a certain amount of money without losing those long-earned federal benefits.

Everett planned a trip to Pennsylvania to test a new antenna that he and his colleagues designed and built. Since I had no clients, I was able to accompany him. We still found each other interesting and fun to be with. As we were driving home, Everett explained the testing results. I shared the new beginning for my book. I would toss out the whole beginning and start fresh.

Then he told me that we would probably move again. Lockheed Martin in Massachusetts would interview him.

"But you hated Massachusetts," I said. "Why would you want to go back there?"

"It's a good, solid job I could do. Besides it's in Marion, Massachusetts, the southern part of the state near the Cape. Probably different from Bolton."

On April, 2005, Everett flew to Massachusetts. I picked him up late at Dulles International Airport. When he got in the car, he told me the interview went well. They would discuss the job candidates and let him know next week if he got the job. Everett was hired and would begin work in May. Our house with the new sunroom went on the market.

One lady came in and walked from the front door to the sunroom and said, "This is the house I want." Her husband insisted they see the rest of the house. They went to the lower level, where Everett had an office and his woodworking shop. The husband said he could turn the shop area into a meeting room. He was a minister and would conduct study classes at home. They left, and another person came through. She liked the house also. Soon there was a bidding war, and we let the realtors handle it. Finally, it was decided to sell to the first couple who looked at it. When they did the final walkthrough the woman said, "That sunroom was what sold me on this home. I love it."

Everett moved to Massachusetts almost immediately and started working. He called to say he found an affordable house in Carver, Massachusetts in a nice neighborhood. There was room for a woodworking shop on the lower floor and office space for me on the main level. By June 5th we officially moved to Carver. Since our belongings wouldn't arrive for several more days, we slept on the floor in the master bedroom until our furniture arrived.

I did not have a job waiting, but there were possibilities in Plymouth, the next town to the east on beautiful Chesapeake Bay. It was going to be interesting living in an area where the first Pilgrams landed, where Thanksgiving began and where Plymouth Rock was on the beach. I was looking forward to exploring all the history there. I also enjoyed seeing expansive cranberry bogs close to our new home.

After getting somewhat settled, I began looking for a part-time job. Soon, I was working for a home health agency in Plymouth owned by Gentiva. I was learning the area as well as getting the opportunity to fill in at an office on Cape Cod. The other OT, who lived on the Cape, was fun to work with. She worked part-time as well, so we often shared clients. If a client needed two or three days of therapy, I would see that client one day and she would see the client the other two days. She preferred to take clients who lived mostly on the Western side of Cape Cod, while I worked with those on the Eastern side of the Cape.

Chapter 50

The Monkey College

One morning, while I was watching the news, I saw a story about a facility that trained monkeys to assist people with quadriplegia. I read an article about Judi Zazula, the woman who trained these Capuchin monkeys, several years before in ADVANCE for Occupational Therapists. I never thought I would be in an area to see Dr. Zazula open a new facility. I was sure that ADVANCE for Occupational Therapists might enjoy a story about the new training center opening near Boston. I called the "Monkey College" to secure a date for a tour and an interview with the director, Judi Zazula. Everett promised to take pictures while I interviewed Dr. Zazula and observed training sessions.

On a Saturday, when Everett and I arrived at the new training center, we were ushered around the facility by one of the trainers. It was a happy, noisy place. We learned that the monkeys must be old enough–usually in the fourth or fifth year of their lives–to begin training. They have a limited work life and need to retire after about twenty years on the job. When they retire, they return to the center where they live out their lives in peace. Monkeys are chatty creatures. They like to move about, given the opportunity, and need a certain amount of exercise every day.

When we were done with the tour, we met Dr. Zazula in the conference room. Her personal monkey, Ayla, joined her. Dr. Zazula uses Ayla to demonstrate to people about how her trained monkeys assist people with spinal cord injuries. While the three of us sat at the table talking, Ayla busied herself taking my many ballpoint pens apart. She did not bother to put them back together before we left, however.

While watching her unscrew the pens, I marveled at her fine motor dexterity, her curiosity and her lengthy attention span. I worked with children who had less attention span than Ayla. Dr. Zazula said that she often took Ayla to the symphony, and Ayla would watch everything, and listen to the music attentively. People would comment on how focused Ayla was on the music and the orchestra. They had no idea that a monkey could be so quiet during a performance. Ayla's focus surprised me, too.

We left the "monkey college" with considerable information and some very nice pictures. I wrote the article and sent it to ADVANCE for Occupational Therapists. Mrs. Brown, the editor, called me when they received my article. She told me she wrote an article about the training of monkeys some twenty years before. Ms. Brown interviewed Dr. Zazula when she first started training monkeys in her own apartment. Some of those monkeys were still caregiving their original "clients". It was fascinating that Dr. Zazula began as an occupational therapist, saw a need, and had the opportunity and foresight to begin this program. I felt honored to write about her achievement. Ms. Brown wrote a short introduction for my article before it was published.

As Dr. Zazula's monkeys only work with people in the New England area they never get as far West as Nebraska. A couple of years ago, in 2019, we happened to see three monkeys in a van in Elk Horn, Nebraska. I made a beeline across the parking lot to see if the owner just had the monkeys for pets, or if they were helper monkeys. I knocked on the window of the van. The driver put the window down a bit. "Hi. I noticed your monkeys. Are they pets?" I asked.

"No. Actually, we train them to assist people with disabilities around here," the driver said.

"Oh. Do you know about Dr. Zazula in Massachusetts? She's been training monkeys for well over twenty years."

"Yes, we do know her. We don't have the kind of facility for training that she does, but we've been to Massachusetts and admired her work. Our training is similar, but we only train about two or three at a time. Her monkeys stay in the New England area. We needed some locally, so my wife and I train Capuchin monkeys for folks in this area. I don't often meet someone who knows about her operation. Happy you stopped by."

"Thank you for the information. I'm glad someone locally is training," I said.

Everett and I left the parking lot with a sense of satisfaction. Thank goodness others trained monkeys to help persons with disabilities. I would love to see that trend spread worldwide.

Chapter 51

Louise

One of my home health clients in Massachusetts was a woman who suffered from severe arthritis, diabetes, and heart problems. A stint was placed in her heart and she was recuperating at home. Years ago, Louise and her husband moved from Minneapolis where he was a surgeon at a large children's hospital. She was a former social worker. They bought a house in downtown Plymouth, just three blocks from the bay. The two had done extensive work customizing their home. However, I was concerned about some of the steps. The steps up from the driveway to the house, and the step up into the living area from the kitchen were difficult for Louise.

A couple of years ago, Louise's husband died. When Louise began having her own debilitating health problems, her daughter, Kathy, moved in with her. Kathy worked full-time at the Plymouth Memorial State Park. So Louise spent most of her days alone.

Louise and I hit it off immediately. She shared stories of her life and was always engaged in reading as well as listening to National Public Radio WGBH from Boston. We both listened to the same programs on NPR and enjoyed some of the same TV programs as well. I made a few housekeeping changes to help Louise. I removed trip-hazard scatter rugs up off her kitchen floor and foyer and had grab bars installed in her bathroom.

One area she wanted to address was driving. She especially wanted to drive to the grocery store and do her own grocery shopping. I agreed with her, but first, we needed to see how mobile she would be in the grocery store. "I was born with a steering wheel in my hands," she often told me. "I'm sure I can drive without any trouble."

"I'm sure you can, but can you walk around the grocery store and carry your items to the car, then bring them into the house and put them away? It's easy enough to drive, but walking might be an issue. I need you to check with your doctor on your next visit to see if you can drive. If he says you can, we'll visit the grocery store."

During her visit to the doctor, he told Louise she could drive.

"On my next visit, I want to see you drive around the block," I said. Louise was not too happy that I was being so cautious, but she assented to my wishes. Louise drove her car briefly. She passed my test. I scheduled the trip to the grocery store for the following week.

Louise was ready to go when I arrived. I assumed she would drive to a grocery store within several blocks from her home. But once she got behind the wheel, she drove onto Highway 3. I realized she was going to a store several miles away.

"I don't like that store near my house. I like the larger store just north of North Plymouth in Kingston," she said.

We arrived at the parking lot, and Louise got a cart out of the rack. She was still using a walker at her house, but she decided the shopping cart would substitute for the walker. I walked along beside her as she pushed the cart into the store. We stopped for fresh vegetables, meat, and a couple of cleaning supplies.

"I can hardly wait to eat something fresh," Louise said. "I'm tired of eating out of cans." About halfway around the store, Louise slowed down and stopped at a little coffee area with tables. "I think I'll have a cup of coffee before we go any farther," she said.

"Sounds good to me." I ordered two coffees while Louise sat at one of the tables. We sat for a while drinking our coffee and chatting.

"I think I just needed to catch my breath," Louise said.

"How do you feel about driving home?" I asked.

"Oh, I'll be fine. You might have to carry the groceries into the house," she said.

"I thought I would. So how do you plan to do that when Kathy, or I, aren't with you?"

"I might just leave them in the car until Kathy comes home, or I'll get myself into the house, rest up, then go get the packages one at a time. Anyway, I know I'll be doing my own grocery shopping from now on."

We finished the grocery shopping tour and returned to Louise's house. I totted the bags in. Louise put away the items she purchased. I wished there had been a grocery-shopping evaluation at that time, like there is now. All I could do was make observations of how Louise drove, how she made decisions and navigated through the grocery aisles. I wrote up my visit and realized that I would be discharging Louise on our next visit. I would miss her. She was spunky and great company.

When I returned to the office, the director of the agency called me into his office. "I understand you were grocery shopping with one of your clients today," he said.

"Yes. It was important to not only see her driving, but also see how she did with shopping."

"Well, you could have gotten into an accident and the liability, or possible law suit could have cost our company considerable money. Don't ever do that again," he ordered. "The other thing I wanted to tell you is that you can't do 'evaluation-only' visits. From now on, you must see patients at least three visits beyond the evaluation, or I'll have to find another OT to do the initial visits."

I left his office with considerable anger roiling inside. Who was he to tell me how to do my job as an occupational therapist. He was a punk kid who had majored in health care management, and he was doing his job, looking out after the company's bottom line. I was doing something far more important: looking out the needs of the patient. And therein lay the conflict. Certainly, this was something I had encountered before. As I calmed down and finished some paperwork, Marsha came over to talk about another patient she had. "I don't want to see this lady anymore, can you take her?"

"I don't know, where does she live?"

"She's out on the Cape, just over the bridge in Sagamore Highlands. She wants to be seen on Thursday afternoon and I have a conflict."

"I think you'd better ask the boss if it's OK. He just read me out about a couple of things, and I don't know how much longer I'll have a job."

"Oh, well the grapevine says that he might not be our boss much longer anyway, but I'll ask him if I can transfer this patient to you." Marsha came back a bit later and told me that the administrator and head nurse allowed her to transfer the woman to me. I was happy to have a reason to visit the Cape. I enjoyed the drive. I could have lunch at a couple of restaurants I liked down that way.

My next visit with Louise included the discharge. "I'm sure going to miss seeing you," I told her as she signed the paperwork.

"I'm going to miss you, too," she replied. I could see Louise was thinking of something as we sat silently for a minute.

"You know," she said, "we could get together for breakfast occasionally. Kathy goes to work early in the morning, and I really don't like eating breakfast alone. It would give me a reason to get up, get going, and have a nice visit with you."

"Oh, I'd love that!" We decided to meet in a couple of weeks at one of the places in Carver where Everett and I liked Saturday breakfasts.

I didn't lose my job after all, but it was close. The manager put me on probation. My workload decreased, and I was not given new patients to evaluate. Marsha was given that duty until she decided to leave the home health agency.

Louise and I continued to see each other for breakfast or lunch about every six weeks or so. Now I was calling her a friend, not a client.

Chapter 52

I Become a Patient Fall 2006

My health had been good in my adult years. I felt very blessed to be in my sixties and had never broken a bone, had heart issues, or diabetes. That was about to change.

There were numerous Hosta plants around our house. Since the Hosta had grown over the walkway at the back of the house as well as in the flower bed along the pool house, I decided to remove most of those plants. There were sticker bushes along the deck of the swimming pool, which I thought were unnecessary, and I planned to dig them out also. As I was removing some Hosta one morning, I pulled hard and my right shoulder popped with sharp pain. I went into the house for some Tylenol, thinking my shoulder had just dislocated and popped back into place with no damage to ligaments.

After several days of continued loss of strength, range of motion, and pain in that shoulder, I decided to get my shoulder checked out by a professional orthopedic specialist. I asked several people who they would recommend and was told about an orthopedic group in Duxbury, just to the north of Plymouth. The group had several specialists in orthopedic surgery. They also managed their own physical therapy clinic.

The earliest appointment was a couple of weeks away, but I decided I'd wait rather than be seen by anyone else. The fellow who specialized in shoulder surgery took one look at my shoulder and said, "You have a torn rotator cuff. We'll do X-rays and an MRI, but I'm sure that's what's wrong."

At the follow-up visit, physical therapy was scheduled for twice a week for six weeks. After that, the doctor wanted a follow-up appointment with him. Of course, he sent me to their clinic, so I would have to make the trip to Duxbury. It was summer anyway and I had quit the home health job, so attending PT easily fit my obligations. I was dutiful in doing the exercises prescribed by the physical therapist. Although I was usually treated by a P.T. Assistant, I did see the P.T. occasionally. After the six weeks, the doctor prescribed another six weeks of therapy. Again I made the trip twice a week.

On my last visit, I was reevaluated by the physical therapist. I had told her earlier that I was not a wimp. She had called me that when she first evaluated me. Still, she should be considerate during her reevaluation. When she asked me to raise my arm as far as I could, and I didn't get it over my head, she seemed to think I was not trying hard enough. She cranked my right shoulder to nearly full range of motion. I winced and told her to stop. I was in extreme pain.

After she finished the evaluation, I returned to the doctor's office, I said I was through with physical therapy. "Well, you seem to have made some progress," he said. I left the office without telling him what had happened in the P.T. clinic during my reevaluation. I thought I might be able to handle things on my own. I continued to do the exercises, but not as consistently as before. I also started to swim at Plymouth Health Club.

Everett and I joined the club so he could get some exercise, and I could swim. A friend taught an aerobics class there. Her classes were usually during the day; however, we went in the evenings. Everett liked to walk the treadmill and lift weights, while I jumped in the pool. My swimming wasn't helping my shoulder much, so I decided to contact the doctor again and talk about surgery.

The surgery date was set for early January. I began preparing for my post-surgical confinement. In good OT fashion, I bought pajamas that buttoned up the front so I wouldn't have to get them on over my head and stress my shoulder. I bought an open-front, extra-large bathrobe that I could put around my right arm, which would be in a sling for several weeks. I knew I wouldn't be driving for at least three weeks, maybe longer. I lined my calendar with visits from several friends at church, those in the neighborhood and other people I knew around Carver and Plymouth, who would come for coffee with me. I arranged the writing group to meet at my house as well. My social schedule was set for after the surgery.

Everett drove me to the hospital in Plymouth. "I'll be here when you wake up." He gave me a kiss and left me in the pre-op area. I observed that there wasn't enough staff to handle the load of patients that morning. When an additional nurse arrived, she was greeted with hugs by the other nurses. She was given some charts. The curtain around where I was lying was closed about that time and I could only hear what was going on after that.

Soon, the anesthesiologist came in and told me what he was going to do and the effects I would feel. I had already gone over all that with my surgeon. The nurse came in and started to "prep" me. She pulled my underwear down and said, "Why do you still have these on?" "Because I wanted them on," I replied. She began swabbing my right hip area. "What are you doing?" I asked.

"Aren't you having a hip replacement?" she said.

"No. I'm having my shoulder repaired," I told her.

Just then, I felt a sharp prick in my neck. The anesthesiologist injected a numbing agent into my neck, and I was out like a light.

When I awoke, my shoulder hurt, and there were two small bandages near the head of my right shoulder muscle, the humerus. When the surgeon entered the post-operation area, he told me that the surgery went well, however, there was much more damage to the ligaments than he had anticipated. "I wish I had done another MRI prior to this surgery," he admitted. I had yet to tell him what I experienced on the last visit with the physical therapist. I don't know why I did not share the information about that tortuous examination with him. Perhaps I didn't trust him, even after the surgery.

I was given a shoulder stabilizing sling to wear for several weeks before my follow-up visit. My scheduled visits from friends and fellow writers went well. The weather turned cold and I was glad to be home, and not able to drive anywhere. My recovery seemed to be progressing well.

It snowed the night before my follow-up appointment. In the morning, I went out to my car and scrapped snow off the windshield before driving over to see the doctor. He came into the examination room and began his check-up. "You are recovering well. You are not to scrape snow off your car," he said.

"Oh, I already did that this morning," I told him. "We don't have a garage at our house."

"I guess I should have told the nurse to call and tell you that you weren't to scrape snow. You will begin twice a week physical therapy starting next week." He began to write the prescription.

"OK. But I'm not going to your P.T," I said emphatically. I proceeded to relate what had occurred at my last clinic visit and why there might have been more damage to my shoulder than he anticipated. I also related what happened in the hospital pre-operational area. The anesthesiologist could verify my story. "I realize," I said, "you all had a very heavy surgical schedule that day and perhaps he won't recall the incident."

"I am sorry to hear this," he said, his eyebrows knitted together. "There is another P.T. in Plymouth who does good work," he said.

"Good. I'll go there. Besides if it's the one at the Plymouth Health Club, we have a membership there, and it is closer to my house."

"That's the one." He handed me the prescription for twice-weekly physical therapy, and I left his office.

My rehabilitation proceeded on schedule. Soon, I was trying to find things to occupy my time besides sitting around the house reading or watching TV. One of my neighbors and I started walking around the neighborhood in the evenings after her work. I did more writing, but nothing that was of much consequence. Then I got a call from the woman who had taken over the directorship of the home health agency. She was a nurse and she begged me to take a couple of patients again. I jumped at the chance.

Chapter 53

More Work Summer, 2007 and into 2008

My first patient was a man with an amputated right leg, just below the knee. During my initial evaluation, he showed me how he maneuvered about at home, and how he dressed and transferred in and out of the shower and on and off the commode. It was obvious he had phantom limb syndrome. This syndrome is distinguished by the feeling that an amputated limb is there and usable. The amputee's brain still feels the amputated part.

Jose and I talked through several strategies. His mind needed to catch up with his body. How he could deal with the sensation of losing his lower leg. Jose had fallen a few times because he was moving too fast and forgot that he no longer had his lower right leg. He was going to have to slow down and think before he started to move out of his wheelchair.

He was not ready for a prosthesis. Like other amputees, he needed enough scar tissue to have a prosthesis fitted.

Together we devised a different routine for his transfers from the wheelchair to other chairs. I also trained his family to politely remind him to use the new strategy. With that, I decided he didn't need my services regularly. I told him I'd call later in the week to see if he was doing OK and not falling anymore. "That sounds good to me," Jose said, sounding relieved that my visits were over.

When I returned to the office, I told the new director that I limited my visit to just the evaluation. "That's OK with me," she said.

"Really?" I was very surprised. "Why is that OK with you, when the last director was ready to fire me for doing evaluations only?"

"Well, first, the old director did not have a medical background. Secondly, he was working for the bottom line and not for the patients. It's important to cooperate with patients. I checked with several of your former clients before I called you back to work. You got good recommendations from those clients," she said.

"Oh, that's nice to hear." I went on to write the report and did not worry about my brief visit and minimal assistance to Jose.

The next several weeks I saw other clients. Then one of the nurses presented an in-service talk on Healing touch. We spent a whole Saturday learning about that expanded technique, which was beginning to receive some substantive research support. Yoga, Tai Chi, acupuncture, and herbal medicine were all blooming as alternatives to traditional pharmaceutical therapies in the West. Medical professions increase research in these areas. The National Institutes of Health began funding more research focusing on these Eastern practices. I was excited to see this turn of events. It seemed to me there had to be some validity to those practices, or they wouldn't have continued for centuries. The Western attitude of scientific evidence in medicine predominated, and yet research on Eastern methods of treatment was necessary.

Besides regular work at the home health clinic, a church friend of mine asked me to babysit her two small children whenever she needed an evening out. Marian was an amateur actress. With rehearsals and then the play, I babysat often. The children were lively, curious, and had a lot of fun. Whenever I could, I took the children to a nearby beach, or to a lake to swim. Sometimes they also come to my house to swim in our pool, too.

The summer of 2008 progressed, and I was enjoying myself. I was beginning to feel settled a bit in our new home. We added new decking on the back porch, and made several other modifications to the home's interior. Then Everett came home and said he was going to look for another job. He felt like he was being treated like a clerk. He wanted to do the design work he was hired to do in the beginning.

Chapter 54

Mrs. Pilkington

One afternoon my OT friend, Martha, called to check on me. "Why don't you come down and visit?" she asked. "Maybe it would take your mind off your constant moves. And I might arrange for you to see the rhododendron farm here on the Cape."

"Oh, that would be great!" Martha had told me about acres and acres of rhododendrons not far from her house on Cape Cod. Mrs. Pilkington, the owner, hybridized and developed several different colors of flowers. Rhododendrons made me think of my childhood. Many people back home in Washington State grew them in their flower beds.

One wet, cold Saturday Everett and I headed to Martha's. We ate a festive lunch with Martha and her husband, then we all went to visit Mrs. Pilkington. She told us about growing up on the Cape, as the daughter of a pharmacist who also grew rhododendrons. Mrs. Pilkington loved gardening even when she was a child. Her gardens were so renowned that people from all over the world came to see her outstanding selections of flowers.

As we walked around the acreage, Mrs. Pilkington explained that the acreage used to be larger. But since she and her husband had grown older, they sold about half of the property. "It just got to be too much," she confided. She pointed out several flower varieties I was familiar with. I told her about working for Weyerhaeuser, Inc. in Washington

State many years ago and the rhododendron garden on their corporate office site.

"Yes, I'm familiar with that. I visited there several years ago," Mrs. Pilkington said. Then I noticed a flower that I had never seen on a rhododendron before. It was purple with a white center. I bent down to read the label.

"Oh, my, this one's named for you!"

"Yes, the Rhododendron Society gave it my name," she admitted, with a slight smile. "We'd better go in, it's beginning to rain harder." She led us back to a large shed and explained how she pollinated and grafted the plants to hybridize colors. She made a point of building in resistance to different insects, also. I listened intently. "How would you like a tray of these?" she asked, pointing to a flat of lilies.

"Oh, that would be lovely," I said. "How much are they?"

"Oh, no. I want to give them to you. Plant them on the west side of your house, in an area that will be partially shaded. They will come back each year if you separate them a bit in the fall."

"Goodness, thank you so much." I glanced over at Martha. She was grinning.

"We'd better get going," Martha said. "It's getting to be a real downpour."

"Thank you for coming," Mrs. Pilkington said. We got into the car, and Martha's husband drove us back to their house.

"I've never seen Mrs. Pilkington take to anyone the way she took to you," Martha said. "She really liked you."

"Oh, I enjoyed her, too. She reminded me of my mother. Willing to get out in all kinds of weather to care for her plants."

We left Martha's soon after our field trip. Driving home to Carver, Everett said he had found several jobs to explore, but nothing in Washington State where most of my family lived. Boeing wasn't hiring, and there didn't seem to be any other local jobs for electrical engineers. "What about Portland or Vancouver?" I asked.

"I'll check those areas, too," he promised.

Chapter 55

One last Home Health Client

Back at the health office, I found a referral for a widow just across the Sagamore Bridge on the Cape. Mrs. Brown lived on a small farm. She had broken her hip. She had learned some rehabilitation techniques in the hospital and was now home. Mrs. Brown needed an evaluation to see how she would do living alone. Her son lived in Boston and only visited once a month. I called to make an appointment with Mrs. Brown on a Tuesday around 10:30 a.m.

When I arrived at Mrs. Brown's house, she opened the front door before I rang the bell.

"Oh, I'm glad to see you," she said. "Please come in. We'll go to the kitchen, where we can sit at the table and my husband can listen in." We walked down a short hall and into the kitchen.

"I understood you were a widow," I said as I sat down at the table.

"Oh, I am. But my husband's ashes are here on the table in that urn," she said. "I don't like eating alone, so I put him there. Sometimes I think I hear him talking to me, but I know he's passed."

I asked a few questions about how she was doing at home, and then we went to her bedroom, where she demonstrated how she got in and out of bed. We went to the bathroom. A grab bar was installed by the toilet and one by the bathtub as well. The laundry was adjacent to the kitchen so she did not have to tote the laundry up and down stairs.

We returned to the kitchen. "What do you think you need help with?" I asked.

"Well, I don't stand long enough to cook, or bake anything," she responded. "I like to take cookies and cakes to church bake sales. I haven't been able to do that since my hip surgery. I don't cook much either. I do like to prepare a nice dinner and sometimes invite a neighbor over to share it. I haven't done that since I've been home either."

"OK. I think if we work on some standing tolerance and maybe some exercises to help with balance, that will be all we need to do. Maybe we can rearrange some things in your cupboards so you won't have to stoop too low. I can also bring you a couple of pieces of equipment that will help you pick things up off the floor or out of the cupboard."

"That sounds good to me," Mrs. Brown said.

I wrote the evaluation report and suggested working with Mrs. Brown twice a week for a month. I thought she would be doing better and feeling more confident in a short time.

The physician agreed and wrote a prescription for OT services.

I returned to Mrs. Brown's home the following Thursday, and we rearranged some skillets and pots in her kitchen. She used the reacher to pick up a couple of things off the floor in her living room. I showed her the stocking aide and also the long-handled shoehorn. She seemed a bit reluctant to use those items but said she would think about it.

We went back to the kitchen and I suggested we play some cards while we stood at the counter. Mrs. Brown thought that was a great idea. She enjoyed playing cards and found it made her standing exercises less boring. Mrs. Brown was determined to increase her stamina. She played Solitaire while standing at the kitchen counter when I wasn't there. She played at least five or six games of Solitaire every day.

On our last appointment date, Mrs. Brown had a plate of cookies on the table. She asked if I would like a cup of coffee, or tea. "Oh, tea would be nice," I replied. I noticed that the urn with Mr. Brown's ashes was no longer on the table. "Where is Mr. Brown? I asked.

"Oh, he was getting in the way when I started baking again. I moved him to the dining room. He's on the little stand by the window. Now that I have company, he doesn't say anything anyway," Mrs. Brown told me. I looked into the dining room. There was the urn in the middle of a small table. There was a potted plant on either side of the urn, one plant was a Christmas cactus, the other a violet. I turned back to the kitchen table and went to sit down.

Mrs. Brown had no trouble filling the teapot with water and placing it on the stove. She also got cups out of the cupboard without any trouble. She moved around her kitchen well. When the teapot whistled, she poured the hot water into our cups and brought them to the table. "See how well I'm doing?" she said. She seemed pleased with her progress.

"Yes. I'm happy everything we've done has helped," I said.

"Thank you. Mr. Brown told me he's happy too, and doesn't have to worry that I'll fall down. I baked a cake and took it to church this past Sunday, too. I'm so glad to be baking and cooking again."

After finishing our tea, she gave me two big chocolate cookies to take home with me. I knew she would be baking for her church. Neighbors would join her for coffee or tea, too. She was back to her usual activities and fun things to do.

Chapter 56

Relocating Again

Everett found a new job in May 2008 in Bloomington, Indiana. The office was downtown, not far from the university campus. He would be doing engineering design work for a company that had contracts with the military.

We put our house in Carver on the market, but this time the real estate market was slow. Possible buyers were scarce. Everett found an apartment in a small town south of Bloomington. He moved there while I stayed in Carver, packing and waiting for the house to sell. In September, I flew to Bloomington just to see the area and look at possible homes to buy. I had never been in the Midwest before and wondered what cultural changes I would encounter. It would be another new learning experience.

While I was in Bloomington, our house in Massachusetts sold and we found a house in Ellettsville, just ten miles from Bloomington. I returned to Massachusetts to arrange for the moving company and schedule repairs on our house before the new owners moved in.

I spent the last months of 2008 getting settled into our house in Ellettsville, Indiana, and finishing a book about Shelton, Washington, for Arcadia Publishing. Then I began looking for classes to take to secure my occupational therapy license in Indiana.

One option was a class in Tai Chi for Arthritis and Fall Prevention and Tai Chi in the Seated Position. Those classes were taught together and would give me enough credit for my license in Indiana. The classes were taught in Indianapolis, about forty-five miles north of Ellettsville at an outpatient clinic. It would be an easy drive since we were on the north side of Ellettsville and the clinic was on the south side of Indianapolis. I enjoyed the directness of interstate driving and could zip up Highway 69/State Road 37.

I applied for those classes. As I wrote earlier, I was delighted that more research was being done on Asian approaches to health care. Tai Chi was one area that was easy and practical for the older population. One of the instructors was an occupational therapy assistant who had been practicing Tai Chi for several years. He also participated in Tai Chi contests. The courses he and another instructor taught were Tai Chi for Health courses developed by Dr. Paul Lam in Australia. Dr. Lam was both Chinese and a physician. His knowledge gave extra weight to the classes he designed. Dr. Lam took up Tai Chi himself while in medical school. He spent his early life in China, where he had little to eat and had to work in the fields. His childhood led to early arthritis. The Tai Chi helped him stay flexible and balanced.

After finishing the classes and receiving my Indiana Occupational Therapy license, I worked two afternoons a week at a nursing facility in Bloomington. They wanted me to teach the Tai Chi for Arthritis in the Seated Position to several residents. One was a Chinese woman who was very arthritic and also had dementia. When I met her, Mrs. C. spoke Chinese more often than English. The Director of the Activities Department thought doing exercises from her own background might help her.

For several months, I went to the facility twice a week and taught Tai Chi for Arthritis in the Seated Position for one hour each session. Six residents, including the Chinese woman, participated. After teaching the class for a while, I noticed that the Chinese woman began skipping classes. The nursing assistant told me that Mrs. C. had difficulty dressing for the class, even though it was in the afternoon. After several more sessions, the Director of the Activities Department told me that my services were no longer needed. Mrs. C. was deteriorating rapidly. She also said that another staff member had just earned her certificate in the same Tai Chi that I was teaching. She would take over the class for the other residents. So, again, I was without a job that paid even a little something.

Besides teaching Tai Chi at the nursing facility in Bloomington, I was doing some volunteer work at the school district in Ellettsville. I enjoyed being with the children. I helped with reading and some handwriting. They were not clients, nor was I getting paid to do that, but I was out and about in the school district. I also went to schools in Bloomington as a volunteer.

I wanted to earn some pocket money again, however.

In the fall of 2010, a faculty position opened at the University of Indianapolis. I applied for it and was hired part-time. My assignment was to co-teach a rehabilitation class. I also taught a pediatric therapy class and an activities class. I was on campus two and a half days a week. After the first semester, I was hired full-time. I was teaching two therapeutic activities classes, a pediatric therapy class and the rehabilitation class on my own. I did not have summer classes, so I began to focus on writing again.

As the University was beginning a Doctor of Occupational Therapy program and expanding their Master's degree in Occupational Therapy, the Department looked for more faculty with doctorates. As they added faculty with doctoral degrees, my teaching schedule shrank. By the end of spring semester of 2013, I was out of a job again. I took some time off to enjoy the summer and decided I would not drive to Indianapolis for a job again, even though the hospital was hiring occupational therapists.

Chapter 57

Tai Chi

During the spring of 2013, I realized that the Senior Center in Ellettsville might welcome a class in Tai Chi. I proposed starting a class two mornings a week to the director. The activities director questioned me about the class Tai Chi for Arthritis. She said she would research it and determine if it would fit. They already had a regular exercise class.

By June, she called and asked me to teach the Tai Chi class. However, I would teach in the afternoon on Tuesday and Thursday. The traditional exercise class would continue in the mornings on Monday and Wednesday. Also, I would only be paid based on the number of students who came to my class. I needed to make Tai Chi as interesting as possible to keep the students.

Five students arrived for the first class. I explained Tai Chi and how it focused on slow, very intense, and structured movements. I taught Tai Chi in a very structured way. I hoped my students would not be bored. I was not permitted to change how I taught, as Dr. Lam's teaching method was part of the certification process. Interestingly, all five students stayed with the class for the eight weeks.

I needed some socialization, so after a couple of classes, I suggested we all meet in Ellettsville after class for coffee at a newly opened coffee shop. The coffee meetings were popular and continued after each class.

The Director of the Senior Center said I could continue teaching Tai Chi for eight weeks in the fall, as well. "I see some dedication in your students. I would like to see you continue, but I will change the time for your class to eight-thirty in the morning on Monday and Wednesday. Your class will be finished by the end of October."

"That sounds OK with me." I was pleased she was willing to continue the class. When we got back together in September, I had a dozen students. I was pleased. This was encouraging. All these additional students stayed with the class. Some of us would go to coffee after the class to enjoy each other's company. All of the students were older, retired women. Some were married with husbands who continued to work. Some of the women were widowed and looked forward to the socialization as well as the gentle exercise.

In the spring of 2014, I continued to teach at the Senior Center, but I noticed that sometimes one or two students were not at class. I added another form called Tai Chi for Diabetes to our program. I began the class with Tai Chi for Arthritis, which all the students knew, and then went on to teach Tai Chi for Diabetes movements, for which I had been newly certified. The students seemed to like learning something new.

Everett was now working out on a military base. The old company had lost contracts, and finished some contract work. Although driving out to the base was a long drive, he had a consistent job. That was a blessing. Everett wanted to update himself. He also planned to start working on a Fundamentals of Engineering license. So, he was busy working and studying.

I decided to look for another part-time occupational therapy job.

Chapter 58

Another Nursing Facility

In the summer of 2014, I interviewed at a nursing home in Ellettsville. All the therapists were employed directly by a national therapy company that contracted with the nursing home. I wanted to work three days a week, but the contract company wanted thirty-two hours a week. We arranged a schedule of three full eight-hour days and two four-hour days. That gave me the 32 hours and a legally full-time schedule. With the new arrangement, I could keep teaching Tai Chi at the Senior Center on my two half days.

I talked with the Director of the Senior Center about changing my schedule to two afternoons a week. She was agreeable. Some of the students in my Tai Chi class could not come in the afternoon, however, most of the long-time students stayed with the class. It turned out that a couple of students had other things come up and could not always attend the afternoon class.

One of the first patients I evaluated at the nursing home that year was a woman who had suffered a stroke. Julia's left arm needed to regain some movement and strength. As Julia was originally left-handed, we also worked on developing more fine motor skills in her right hand and arm. With additional strength, she could use both her right or left hand for activities of daily living, such as feeding herself, brushing her teeth, and buttoning her clothes. I worked with Julia three times a week.

Julia loved to listen to classical music. I suggested to her daughter that she bring her mother a CD player so she could listen to music all the time rather than rely on erratic selections from the public radio station. Her daughter thought that was a good idea and soon Julia had a CD player in her room and a number of discs to play.

As Julia and I worked together, I noticed that she seemed to be losing some of her short-term memory. I talked with the nursing staff during a clinical meeting, and it was determined that Julia needed an evaluation for possible Alzheimer's disease. A physician diagnosed Julia with a rapid decline in cognitive function and memory.

One day, I went into Julia's room, and she spoke in a language I did not understand. After calling her daughter, Christine, and discussing what happened, Christine told me that Julia was Jewish. She sometimes spoke in Hebrew. Julia was born into a Jewish family overseas, and when they moved to the United States in the late 1940s, the family only spoke English. After all this time, the language had revived. Christine shared that Julia studied to be a concert pianist before World War II started. After the war the family moved to the United States.

When Julia met her husband and married, they moved to Indiana. After her husband died, Julia became depressed and then had the stroke. Her daughter was an only child, and because she had a full-time job, Christine decided that Julia would have better care in the nursing home. She was also aware that Julia was declining rapidly.

One of the things that Julia loved to do was walk outside. Sometimes she would go outside the nursing facility without an escort. I was concerned that she might walk up the road into highway traffic.

"She loves to watch birds. She had several bird feeders at our house. Maybe she's looking for birds," Christine confided.

"OK. I'll get a feeder and have it put outside her room window. That way she can safely stay in her room and watch the birds at the feeder. How would that be?"

Christine loved the idea. That afternoon, when I got off work, I went to the farm store not far from the facility. I bought a feeder and some bird seed. When I went to work the following day, I talked to the janitor about putting the feeder, with seed in it, outside Julia's back window. Later in the afternoon, the feeder was where I wanted it to be. A bird was already on the feeder eating.

"Julia, come over here," I said. She got up from her chair and came to the window. She saw the bird on the feeder and smiled brightly. "Now you don't have to go outside to see birds."

I left and Julia never went outside without an escort after that to my knowledge. I called Christine and asked if Julia would like a visit from the Rabbi in Bloomington. She did not think her mother would appreciate that. "When I was growing up, neither she, nor my dad, ever wanted to be known as Jewish. Only the family knew that. I'm not sure I should have told you, either."

"OK. I won't share that with anyone either. I'm just glad that your mother is staying in her room to watch the birds and doesn't wander up the road anymore."

Chapter 59

The End of my OT Career

The speech therapist and I were working with Sandra. We were helping her with her feeding skills. Sandra was a stroke patient. She had difficulty speaking, swallowing and feeding herself. All were factors typical of patients with severe strokes on the left side of the brain. Sandra tried to talk, but her tongue and lip movements were inconsistent and a bit beyond her control.

One day at lunch, I was working with Sandra without the speech therapist. Sandra put a spoonful of thickened clam chowder into her mouth. She did not swallow it, but kept moving her tongue around. I realized something was in her mouth that she could not, or would not swallow. I told her to spit whatever was in her mouth onto a napkin. She looked at me as though she did not want to do that, but I told her it was OK to spit whatever it was out. She finally did.

There on the napkin was a fairly large piece of plastic, apparently from the top of a bottle. I asked an aide to help Sandra eat, and I went to the kitchen to talk to the cook. "I have been working with Sandra at lunch and this is what was in her chowder. What is it?"

"Oh, that's off a milk carton. It must have fallen into the chowder by mistake. It sometimes happens." He seemed not at all concerned.

I went to the director of the facility, and showed him the plastic top. "The cook said that these things sometimes fall into food. What if a patient swallowed it. That could be a real problem. Aren't you concerned? Shouldn't the cook be checking on these things before serving food to the residents?"

"Oh, it does happen, but not very often. I wouldn't worry about it. Sandra didn't swallow it, so no problem."

I was livid. I decided then and there that I would no longer work for a facility with such an uncaring attitude. I turned in my resignation.

The head of the therapy department, came to see me on my last day. "Won't you consider working on an on-call basis?" she said.

"Only if I never have to work with someone in the dining room again without the help of another therapist and have access to a strainer to check soups or liquids," I replied.

"OK. I promise. I'll have our other OT work with those patients."

I ended up working for another six weeks on-call. I worked exclusively with a gentleman with Alzheimer's Syndrome.

Chapter 60

Another Move

Everett passed the test for his Professional Engineering license and found a job in Nebraska. We moved in 2016, and I decided not to apply for an occupational therapy license in Nebraska. I had just turned seventy-six, and I wanted to write. Within a year, I was accepted to the University of Nebraska-Omaha Creative Writing Program for a Master of Fine Arts in Writing. That ended my career as an occupational therapist and as a university faculty member.

The OT profession grew and progressed. Many occupational therapists were completing doctorates. There are still occupational therapy assistants with lesser degrees. A number of new regulations and techniques have also been introduced. I have not kept up.

When my book, *ALASKA STORIES: A Memoir,* was published, I returned to the University of Puget Sound in Tacoma, Washington. The director of the occupational therapy program asked me to talk about my experiences in Alaska. I outlined remarks to share with their OT students and faculty.

I did several things as an OT that I probably should never have done. One was to have a six-year-old girl come to stay at my home in Tacoma over a weekend. I wanted to see how she would do in an environment outside the clinic. Her parents thought that was a good idea, too. Her mother brought her to my house on a Friday evening and after visiting for a while, she left. During the weekend, the child and I fixed meals together, went grocery shopping, and attended church on Sunday. I was able to see the child in a different light and provide helpful suggestions after that weekend.

Another incident was having my patient in New Mexico come to mow my lawn and have lunch with me at my house. I don't know of any other therapist that would do such a thing. But again, I gained some insight into how that young man behaved.

I would not suggest that a therapist ever do these kinds of things now. Professional standards these days require more distance. However, just interviewing parents about a child's behavior outside the school, or clinic is helpful and often still a part of the OT interview process.

I continue to talk about occupational therapy to people I meet, especially to young people who are looking for an interesting career. Occupational Therapy helps so many people with illnesses and disabilities. Insight, work, and tenacity can turn lives around for the better. I was very fortunate to have such an amazing career and rewarding clients. I was lucky to travel to so many places, literally from one end of the country to the other. I experienced a variety of cultures and learned so much. I treasure all I learned and enjoyed so many of the people I worked with.

The End

www.ingramcontent.com/pod-product-compliance
Ingram Content Group UK Ltd.
Pitfield, Milton Keynes, MK11 3LW, UK
UKHW062255290726
14090UKWH00017B/711

9 798896 396338